Praise for

All Goodbyes Aren't Gone

"You can always count on Ann Jeffries for a good story, great characters, and a few surprises! All Goodbyes Aren't Gone doesn't disappoint!" J.A. Meinecke, Author, *A Woman to Reckon With*

"Once again Ann Jeffries created complex characters with a riveting story line. The escapades of this fictional family continue to amaze and inspire me. So when is Ms. Jeffries going to write a Family Cookbook? I'll be first in line to purchase one if she does." Rebecca Bridges, Author, After the Reunion

"Ann Jeffries wields another multi-layered tale of two professionals looking for a new start and finding it in the most interesting places. She purposefully weaves characters throughout the piece to show just how connected this family is and the lengths they are willing to go for one another. This is yet another testament to Ms. Jeffries' talents as a writer." L.S. Casey, Author, *Alma Mater and Night Watch.*

"I did not want this story to end! I love Ann Jeffries' characters, their interactions, and wish to be part of such a beautifully loving large family! The pages flowed with equal parts of intrigue and romance. Her descriptions paint clear pictures and my mouth waters when I read about the food! Excellent and left wanting for more and soon!" Barb Ryan, Author

"Ann Jeffries has written an original and authentic love story that avoids all the usual clichés and thoroughly involves the reader in the lives of two appealing and beautiful people." Abe Leib, Esquire

All Goodbyes Aren't Gone

Another Family Reunion Novel
In The Wisdom of the Ancestors Series

ANN JEFFRIES

Copyright © 2017 by Ann Jeffries
www.annjeffries.net
All rights reserved
Printed and Bound in the United States of America

Published and Distributed By
New View Literature
820 67th Avenue N, #7603
Myrtle Beach, South Carolina 29572
www.newviewliterature.com

Editorial Services:
Laurie D. Willis, Owner
Laurie's Write Touch!

Interior and Cover design:
Jessica Tilles
www.TWASolutions.com

ISBN: 978-1-941603-01-7 Print
ISBN: 978-1-941603-62-8 eBook

Library of Congress Control Number: 2014909737
First printing August 2017

This is a work of fiction. Names, characters, businesses, places, events and incidents are either the products of the author's imagination or used in a fictitious manner. Any resemblance to actual persons, living or dead, or actual events is purely coincidental.

No part of this book may be reproduced, stored in a retrieval system or transmitted in any form or by any means without the prior written permission of the publisher—except by a reviewer who may quote brief passages in a review to be printed in a newspaper, magazine or journal.
For inquires, contact the publisher.

Acknowledgements

I bow in humble appreciation to:

The Creator

My Ancestors

Laurie D. Willis
www.laurieswritetouch.com

Abe Leib, Esq., Mentor

Jessica Tilles, Interior and cover design

The Carolina Forest Authors' Group

Carolina Forest Public Library, Horry County, SC

My extraordinary son, Ted Jeffries, for the many wonderful years of basketball memories

Family, friends, and fans

The journey continues and the struggle for literary perfection shall never end.

I remain faithfully yours,

Ann Jeffries

Other Ann Jeffries Titles

In the Family Reunion—Wisdom of the Ancestors Series:

Southern Exposures

Another Point of View

Northern Exposures

Uncommon Choices

An Unguarded Moment

Moments To Remember

The Better Part of Valor

Walking on Uneven Ground

Ask Me No Questions . . . I'll Tell You No Lies

Touch Me In The Morning

All Goodbyes Aren't Gone

It's been a long time

Every bit of yesterday

You've been on my mind

Every minute you were away

—*Johnny Bristol, All Goodbyes Aren't Gone*

Prologue

It was the last game of the series, the last game of the season, and likely the last game of his illustrious, professional career, thought Gregory Clayton Alexander. The press and news media, when they learned from his bio his family actually descended from Alexandria, Egypt, founded by the Alexander III of Macedon, they tagged him with the name Alexander the Great during his first year in college. When his name and number were called loudly with verve by the announcer in the SRO Madison Square Garden arena, using that tag line, he winced, but he stood and trotted to center court through the Soul-Train path lined by his teammates.

The boisterous crowd erupted; the roar so loud it was deafening.

He played his entire seven years of professional basketball here with the same team; people he both liked and respected. Not just friends and fans, but people he regarded as family. He set impressive record-breaking stats, never failing to score in the triple double digits, earned two Olympic Gold Medals, and two NBA Championship rings to show for his time in uniform and potentially a third if they could clinch the title tonight. It was a brutally, hard fought series tied three all. The adrenalin rush was flowing and their team was pumped to make this last game historic. Mentally and emotionally, he was immersed in his zone outside of time and space.

The adulation he received didn't die down and even the opposing team and coaches stood and applauded. However, he couldn't deny the way it made him feel to see his parents, siblings, nieces, nephews, aunts, uncles, cousins; an entire tier of family and close friends from home and elsewhere stacked in the stands; his personal rooting section standing up for him with banners proclaiming him as theirs. For just a moment his heart was so full, it brought tears to his eyes. He tapped his heart three times with a closed fist and then pointed to his family, but he had to keep his head in the game. He knew there would be a ceremony to retire his number 42 jersey following the game regardless of who won the season title. He had been through the retirement of his jersey before in high school in Goodwill, Summer County, South Carolina, and then again in college, at the University of Virginia, but this would be the very last one for the rest of his life.

Gregory Clayton Alexander would not be a man afraid to face his future once the cheering stopped.

Though he resented the tagline "Alexander the Great" used liberally during interview, he agreed to speak on camera with ESPN, ABC, CBS and NBC and to be interviewed after the game by a few other regional sports' programming networks. His agent was approached to have him say, when asked by a reporter what he would be doing next, he was to say he was going to Disney World. He easily rejected the contract. Actually, all he wanted was to escape the hype and spend some quality time with his family, particularly his younger sister, Aretha Grace, at the private party his family planned for later. Since the very beginning of his early childhood experience playing basketball in his hometown, Aretha was his taliswoman. She helped him workout, exercise, practice, and study on a daily basis. A lot of his success he owed to her unfailing support.

He also had some big shoes to fill. His father, Dr. Bernard Alexander, played basketball at Howard University on an athletic scholarship. His two older brothers, Kenneth and Benjamin, both played in college and turned down opportunities to play professionally. Twin cousins, Donald and James Dixon, both had stellar athletic collegiate careers, and even his older sister, Vivian Lynn, now a US Appellate Court Judge, also played on a winning US Olympic team while a student at Spelman College. Out of thirty or so first cousins, only a few didn't play the game in high school and college.

Basketball was in his family's DNA, the majority of whom, both male and female, were tall and athletic. Better still, Gregory and his cousins could have attended any number of colleges or universities on academic or athletic scholarships. Though others had the opportunity, he was the only one in his family's history to accept an NBA contract; to take the road less traveled seven years ago. It was gratifying to learn yesterday from his agent that he would be inducted into the basketball Hall of Fame this year. He had enjoyed the game, but now, after playing more than eighty professional games a season for seven years, it was time to end this chapter of his life. He was trading in his NBA career to put his MBA to work as a founding partner in a new, stock-and-bond, brokerage firm. Alexander, Chandler, Jackson, Lightfoot, McAlister and Montgomery, PA, constituted Compliant Trading and Investment, Inc., (CTI), a newly seated Wall Street brokerage house, banking institution, business insurance underwriters, and member of the New York Stock Exchange.

The partners were loosely connected as friends and some as relatives. Margo Chandler was his agent's, Bill Chandler's, sister; Troy Jackson was Vivian's brother-in-law of her first husband; Jeremy Lightfoot was the brother of another one of Vivian's law partners, Alan Lightfoot, Attorney General for the recently created United Native American Nation; China McAlister was one of Vivian's former client's comptroller and business associates; and Joyce Montgomery was Vivian's current husband's sister. Joyce and Troy were also related through their siblings. Joyce's older brother, Bob, and Troy's sister, Sheila were husband and wife.

They had solid academic backgrounds and gained valuable experience working in various aspects of the financial industry. The collaboration of their combined talents gave them a promising start and a leg up over their competitors. They were the young titans looking to quickly expand their talent base with the addition of a few more partners. They offered partnerships to Jackson Chase, a well-known, commodities trader taking the industry by storm and Adam Atterly, a west-coast trader showing incredible savvy in the insurance market who happened to be Gregory's cousin's, James Dixon's, brother-in-law.

When Gregory announced his retirement from professional sports at the end of his current contract to embark fulltime upon this new career, no one, outside of his family and close friends, understood or wanted him to quit. After all, he was not even thirty yet. His agent, Attorney William Chandler, was inundated with offers of ridiculously outrageous sums of money for him to continue to play for other teams in the league; some offering a percentage of the team as an inducement. What they didn't know or understand was he already owned a percentage of his current team. So, it wasn't about the money. He had more than enough to sustain his lifestyle and the means of generating more wealth if he chose to. For him, it was about completing a goal set in his childhood and starting on another challenging one.

He remembered one Labor Day holiday when he was still just a kid. It was when he decided what he wanted to do with his life in the short term. He, his siblings, and about thirty of his first cousins were camped out in tents on the beach in front of their great-grandaunt Hannah Ivy Benson's house. It was the crack of dawn and they were laughing about and recounting one of his brother's, Benny's, sexual escapades when his cousin James asked him,

"You are practicing safe sex, right, Greg?"

"I wouldn't call it practice, exactly," he answered and grinned smugly, *"but, yeah, I remember what y'all taught me."*

"Oh, so you think you've got pro status now, huh?" Benny asked.

"World class."

"It's your responsibility, Benny. You handle it," Kenneth directed.

Benjamin's long-suffering sigh was audible before he sat up, took off his sunglasses, and looked him in the eyes. *"Look, G, I think you missed the moral of my story."*

"Oh, I got it all right," he recalled saying and laughing. *"I won't ask a hunnie dip to marry me until after I'm making big, stupid money. Then she'll think twice before she refuses. Everybody knows there ain't no romance without finance. Ain't no love without the glove,"* he said and, at the time, believed it as if those were two of the Ten Commandments.

"Greg," Benny said, shaking his head in frustration, *"we're definitely going to have a little talk before I leave to go back to the Air Force Academy."*

"You still thinking about playing pro ball?" Donald asked him.

"Only for a little while. After I get in and make some money, I want to go into business for myself just like James wants to do."

"Doing what?" James asked.

"Stocks and bonds. Investments, financial planning. Something like it," he answered at the time. "Uncle Calvin works on Wall Street and when I went to visit him he said there is a lot he could teach me about working in the financial markets."

"He's a good teacher, too," Kenneth added.

His parents and grandparents taught him and his four siblings to set goals and adhere to the family principles: essentially, each one teach one. Every year for a week surrounding the Fourth of July holiday hundreds of his family members converge on Goodwill, Summer County, South Carolina, in reunion of mind, body, and spirit. They came together to rededicate their lives to the wisdom their ancestors passed down through the ages of their family and to ensure the success of future generations.

In addition, each Labor Day holiday at summer's end, the young cousins still in schools follow the family tradition and continue gathering at great-grandaunt Hanna Ivy's house at Atlantic Beach on the South Carolina Grand Strand to offer moral support for the academic year ahead.

He had a great childhood growing up among family and friends on their farm; a good academic career through both undergrad and the year of graduate school; and a professional career that made him wealthy and, he hoped, wise. He finished undergrad in three years and grad in one. Still he had no one special to share his life with. He had dated heavily in college and after, but found no relationship hit all of his buttons. Along the way he lost his cocky, childhood attitude toward women and sex. He wanted much more at this juncture in his life. His parents' and three of his siblings' successful marriages were his role models. He would not settle for anything less successful for himself; he never had. The next phase of his life was just beginning and, to his mind, just as challenging as the last.

In Paris, France, Angelique Teresa Menendez-Gaza took to the runway wearing a snow-flake white wedding gown creation by Carlos Ortega with the panache of the consummate professional she was since age eleven. She was soon to be twenty-one and ready to close this chapter of her life. She and her younger brother, Miguel, both became high-dollar earners in the movie, fashion, and beauty industries before they hit puberty. They had a certain exotic Latin look and appeal the fashion houses, advertising agencies, and movie producers were looking for at an opportune moment. Fortunately, they had the right representation in their agent and attorney, William Chandler. He used his renowned legal skills to cut the best deals for them, while ensuring their childhoods were as normal as possible.

William, Bill to his friends, and Chandler to the world of high fashion, once lived the life of a fledgling model, too, and, on occasion, still did, so he understood what was necessary to be a success in a tough industry. Regrettably, at a young age he had no one to look out for his welfare. Instead, because of his extraordinary good looks, his parents pimped him out to any pervert with the price of a date in his pocket. Before he was fourteen, Bill booked his own dates with a regular clientele and, after he dumped his parents and became emancipated, his modeling career skyrocketed. When one client, a particularly brutal, older man demanded exclusivity or else, Bill wisely dropped out of the life and off the circuit, went to college at Columbia University, and, later, law school at Georgetown. He was wealthy by then and during his early summer days in an advanced scholars' program his first year at Georgetown Law, he met Vivian Alexander, a fellow advanced scholar law student. She had rooms to rent in her brother's huge nearby brownstone on the edge of Washington's Rock Creek Park. Though he could afford to live anywhere, he moved into the house with her and other law students in the scholars program. He marked it as the first of the best days of his life.

Angelique felt the same as Bill about Vivian because it was Vivian who found her, her mother, Anna, and her younger brother, Miguel, destitute and living in a family homeless shelter days after a record-breaking snow storm. Vivian and other law school students were shelter volunteers helping the residents with whatever they needed to improve their situations. Angelique and her family journeyed from Peru to search for their father, Anna's husband, who had abruptly stopped sending messages and money home more than six months earlier. What they found when they finally got to Washington, DC, three months later was a burned-out building where men had lost their lives. Suffering a great disappointment, destitute, and on the verge of malnutrition, starvation, and dehydration, Angelique contracted scarlett fever and was near death when Dr. Chuck Montgomery, who had come looking for Vivian at the homeless shelter, noticed she was ill and rushed her to medical care with his friend, Dr. Derrick Jackson, a renowned pediatrician and pediatric surgeon. Vivian and another law school student, Alan Lightfoot, accompanied them to Dr. Jackson's office.

That chance meeting between Dr. Jackson, a former basketball Gold Medalist, icon and multi-billionaire, and Vivian led to their marriage after she graduated from law school and passed the bar exam. Unfortunately, Derrick, more than ten years Vivian's senior, died less than a year after they married, leaving her one of the wealthiest young women in the world. Nevertheless, Angelique believed Vivian Alexander and Chuck Montgomery actually saved her life that day in the homeless shelter and offered her, Miguel, and their mother a whole new lease on life. Vivian and Chuck took her and her family to live in the Georgetown house with the seven law school housemates who became her surrogate family.

Angelique reached the end of the runway, and then stood for a dramatic moment in practiced pose like a fixed-stare mannequin while the audience cheered wildly. She robotically, slowly brought her fingers to her lips then flung a kiss to the crowd from her right slowly and smoothly pivoting on the balls of her feet to her left completing a three-hundred-sixty-degree circle as if on a rotating platform. She'd given her heart to her craft as a super model and spokesperson for many causes, but this would be her last performance. She turned completely around and took her last mannequin-like, moon walk backward toward the curtain swaying her hips in her signature prance. She smiled to her right and to her left with arms outstretched and palms open and up. She reached the curtain, looked at her audience one last time standing in jubilant adoration and then in a dramatic puff of white sparkling smoke, flash of strobe lights, and a dramatic music crescendo. Everything stopped and she seemed to have just vanished.

The stage craft for her final appearance was timed perfectly. She was mobbed the moment she made it through the curtain to back stage, but she immediately disrobed. Ardon, another supermodel and dear friend, whispered good luck to her, but the show had to go on. The famous designer, Carlos Ortega, entered the stage through the residual smoke with all of the other models except her. Overhead, the wedding gown Angelique wore for her final appearance was on a robotic mannequin of her likeness being smoothly hoisted toward the makeshift heavens with flashing laser lights and dramatic music.

Angel, her stage name, had risen.

Wasting no time backstage, Angelique quickly erased any sign of makeup, dressed in a man's wardrobe complete with a hat to hide her too easily recognizable hair, and slipped into the audience unnoticed. Everyone would be waiting for autographs and pictures at the stage door, while she drifted undetected out the front door among the crush of humanity. She knew Stanton Durant, III, would be waiting among the crowd at the stage entrance. She tried to end it with him as equitably and amicably as possible, but he was insistent their relationship was not over. In point of fact, for her, it had never started.

When she slipped into one of the many taxicabs lined up at the fashion house, she noted Stanton was, indeed, standing outside his limo, a bouquet of exotic flowers in hand, bobbing and weaving looking for her while cataloging everyone who left. Her regular driver had instructions to stay by the stage door until the crowds dissipated giving the illusion she was still inside. By the time everyone left, she would already be in the air headed for the United States.

She pulled the brim of the hat lower, turned away from the chaotic sight, and instructed the cabby to take her to the Charles de Gaulle Aéroports de Paris.

A while later, at the private jetport entrance, not surprisingly her eighteen-year-old brother, Miguel, awaited her. He joined her in being incognito. His many starring movie roles, his recurring role on a popular television soap opera, and appearances on the covers of many fashion magazines made his face easily recognizable. He was recently approached by an executive producer who was developing a primetime police action drama; a revival of New York Undercover. Miguel was being asked to assume the role of Eddie Torres; one previously played by the actor Michael DeLorenzo. Because of his similarity to the actor and youthful good looks they wanted him to play one of the leading roles as an undercover cop particularly in high school or college-related crime episodes. He could carry such a role because of his thick, black hair he wore loose to his shoulders. It tended to wave and curl around a cherubic face still smooth and unblemished. Miguel and DeLorenzo both had hair and facial features in common and looked much younger than their chronological ages.

"You were unbelievable tonight," Miguel said, as he hugged his older sister and kissed her forehead. "Your robotic moves are always perfect. I really liked the last bit of showmanship, too, but you're really rockin' this Victor/Victoria look."

"Thank you," she said, and gave him an extra squeeze, "I think. I'm surprised you made it here from Italy in time to see the show. I spotted you in the audience. You must have wrapped your movie early." He was younger, but taller than her five-foot, ten-inch frame by almost a half-foot she noticed as they hugged before walking toward the Customs Officer. Their luggage was already on board the private Adventurer Executive Airline jet and the pilots were merely awaiting their arrival for the next leg of their journey. They would fly from Paris, France, to Washington, DC, to spend time with their mother, Anna, who in the last years married Fenster Jones, a world renowned concert violinist. He regularly performed with the Washington Symphony Orchestra, though he traveled extensively for solo performances before packed music halls and theatres and lived quietly next door to them in the Georgetown house.

Fenster actually taught piano and violin to her and Miguel from the time they first came to live in Vivian's house next door as preadolescent children. Angelique was quite an accomplished pianist as a result; however, Miguel migrated from the violin to the guitar and toyed with the idea of starting a band to add to his growing repertoire of talents.

Years after the fire and police departments concluded their investigations, reporting Miguel Menendez-Gaza, Sr., perished in the purposefully-set, rooming-house fire, his still young wife, Anna, became an American citizen as did Angelique and Miguel, Jr. Though they still had relatives in Peru, whom they visited at least once a year, they now claimed America as their homeland. Anna and Fenster, a talented, but shy man, ten years her senior, dated for several years before she finally agreed to be his wife. Both Angelique and Miguel were thrilled for the still relatively young couple and they all moved into Fenster's five-bedroom home. Anna remained the majordomo of Vivian's household next door even after Vivian first married Dr. Derrick Jackson and, after his death, then much later married Dr. Charles Montgomery.

Angelique was, at a very early age, infatuated with Vivian's younger brother, Gregory Clayton Alexander, who would come to Washington to work during summer breaks while still in high school or in college at UVA. She, Gregory, and his younger sister, Aretha Grace, became close friends with Joyce Montgomery and Margo Chandler while she was in high school. Her modeling and movie careers often took her away and left her little time to continue cultivating a relationship with Gregory.

However, it wasn't unusual for Gregory to invite her and Chuck's sister, Joyce Montgomery, a student at The American University, to come to Charlottesville for tailgate parties and football and/or basketball games on weekends. Usually Bill's sister, Margo, who was older than Joyce by a few years, would drive them down to Charlottesville, Virginia, to visit

Gregory on campus. Aretha, who was also still in high school, had a pilot's license from the age of thirteen, would arrange to fly up from Goodwill, South Carolina, to join them.

Regrettably, Gregory, a very handsome and affable young man, did not lack for female attention. In fact, Angelique's cousin, Carmen Menendez-Gaza, also a University of Virginia student and Gregory seriously dated for more than a year. Angelique had to say goodbye to her youthful fantasies about having a more intimate relationship with Gregory. She went on to date other young men; however, none lived up to her estimation of to Gregory Alexander. So many of them got off on the idea of dating a super model whose face and physique regularly graced on some of the top magazines, movie screens, television ads, and billboards everywhere. Still others thought of her as having a body-by-Fischer-and-a-brain-by-Mattel mentality. With the conclusion of her last performance, the fast-paced, jet-set existence was at an end. Between career opportunities, she completed the Le Cordon Bleu curriculum. Now, with her extraordinary resources and fame, she would open what she hoped would be her first five-star restaurant, Angelique's Place, next month in one of the most challenging restaurant markets, New York City. Attached to the restaurant, she would open The Run Way, a night spot for an up-scale clientele who wanted to see and be seen. The entrance would actually be a stage so those entering would make their debut as faux models and be photographed.

The venues just happened to be in the same city where Gregory Alexander lives.

"What's on your mind, Angel?" Miguel asked.

Pulling out of her malaise, she gave her brother a distracted smile, took off her hat, tossed it aside, and shook out her long, thick, lustrous, black hair. "The restaurant," she said.

"Problems?" he asked, his brows furrowed in concern.

She shook her head. "No, not really. I'm just wondering whether I'm ready for this."

"You know if you need more capital, I'll help."

She knew he would and had. He was a good friend and loving brother. They were close siblings. "Thanks, but you're already my investor."

"Hey, that way I always know where I can get a good meal," he teased.

"More like a free meal," she said, and laughed.

"Either you or *momi* will always make sure I have a place at the table."

He was right about it. From the time they emigrated from Peru, Anna Menendez-Gaza cooked, cleaned, and ran the household for the law school students living in the huge Georgetown townhouse, and provided, with the housemates' help, a safe and secure environment in which to grow up. The housemates appreciated Anna's efforts and demonstrated affection for her, Angelique, and Miguel by buying gifts for them, clothes and shoes, taking them on trips, paying for them to attend private schools, taking care of their medical bills and health care needs, and generally treating them like family. Bill Chandler arranged to get Miguel his first contract with a top designer and fashion house at age seven which led to contracts for her as well. Even all these years later, the original Menendez-Gaza family wanted for nothing. Their stepfather was a wonderful man and provider. He doted on their mother and treated them as if they were his own naturally born children.

"I noticed the third Stanton Durant was at the show tonight."

She shrugged. "Don't make anything of it. The press and news media are doing enough of that as it is. His family made it clear last year in Majorca, Spain, they would never permit their blue-blooded son and only heir to marry an untitled commoner from Peru. I was perfectly fine to sleep with or to become his mistress, but I was told by his father not to believe he would ever be permitted to marry me. The Senior is still a member of the British House of Lords."

"Little did they know you never slept with the Third and it was you who refused often and continuously to consider marriage to him," Miguel said, with a contentious frown and huff.

"Yeah, go figure," she deadpanned as the Adventurer Executive Airline jet left Parisian airspace carrying its two passengers and three crew members back to the United States.

Chapter 1

Sweat dripped down Gregory's extremely well-toned body leaving a salty sheen in its wake. This was the fifth game of twenty-one points of the day and the opposing team was a bit younger and more agile. It had been nearly six months since his last professional game, but he felt like it was his first. Three times a week he played with a bunch of former pro and talented amateur basketball players with current careers in the financial industry. The talent on the hardwood easily represented a couple of billion in clientele. Some people settled for the three-martini-lunch crowd or eighteen holes of golf, but Gregory and his pals went for the extreme exercise and competition on the hardwood.

Two teams of two women and three men battled on the gleaming hardwood while another five equally talented players sat the bench of the exclusive health and sports club, Indulgences, in midtown Manhattan, waiting their turn to score. Everyone got a chance to play and take on all comers until they lost a game. Five games were going on simultaneously. In this round-robin, they were paired against a very talented team. A win was needed by Gregory's team to advance another notch on the club's leaders' board. Right now they were in fifth place tied with two other teams.

Alondra Martin, a Gold Medal winner out of Michigan State University and former Arizona pro basketball player, now a bank vice president, was making that goal difficult. She had a deadly three-point shot and she was working it like it was her regular nine to five. Her team was down in the ranking and not in contention with the teams in the top ten. At that moment Gregory dearly wished his sister, Vivian, was on his team, but neither love nor money would induce her to miss the first Monday in October, opening day of the US Supreme Court's deliberations.

A judge on the US Appellate Court for the District of Columbia, his sister enjoyed watching the first day of the high court each year and dreamed of one day serving as a Supreme Court Justice. She played regularly in Washington, DC, with Final Justice; a team of female law students, lawyers, and judges. He knew, even as good as Alondra was, she would be no match for Vivian's skills and abilities on the basketball court. His sister had a Gold Medal, too, and rejected opportunities to play professionally domestically and abroad.

Gregory dropped back to cover his man one-on-one and smoothly pivoted to provide back up when he saw his team member, Lori Roberts, put a hand up in Alondra's face to block her view to the basket. Nevertheless, Alondra's potential, three-point shot went up headed unerringly for the bottom of the bucket when Jackson Chase leapt, hand outstretched, and batted the ball away.

The head referee's whistle blew and a goaltending charge was leveled on Jackson's play. When the referee counted the three-points, it ended Greg's team's win streak at 21-20 points only winning four of five games for the day. They were still in contention for the top five on the leaders' board.

Nevertheless, in the spirit of good sportsmanship, both teams lined up to shake hands.

"Hi, handsome. You got plans for tonight?" Alondra asked, following Gregory as he walked off the court while the next team and Alondra's team again warmed up preparing to do battle.

" 'Handsome'," he repeated and snorted out a derisive grunt. He pulled his iPhone from his duffle to check his calendar. Frowning as he thumbed through he noted he was scheduled to go to the theatre with Jackson Chase that night; a plan he had forgotten about. "I do, yes. Why, what did you have in mind?"

She stood hip shot with a basketball under her left arm against her damp uniform jersey and shrugged. "Dinner. There's a new restaurant I want to try. I finally got reservations for five today."

"That'll work if it's at five, and, if you want, you could come with me and Jackson Chase to see this show opening on Broadway at eight?"

"Date. I'll meet you at your office at five. We can share a car."

"Done," he said, as they bumped fists and parted ways. He hefted his duffle and headed for the showers and sauna while Alondra dribbled the ball back onto the hardwood and shot it from near mid-court making another three-point basket.

After his shower and sauna, Gregory headed for the massage rooms.

"This way, Mr. Alexander," an attendant instructed as soon as Gregory entered. It amazed him people knew him on sight. He understood his six-ten height set him apart when he was not around his equally-tall family members, but still to be recognized by his face in his mind was surprising. The attendant showed him to the large, heated pool where men reclined on half submerged tables in the steamy, heated water to a space next to Jackson Chase and provided an ice-cold bottle of water.

"We still on for tonight?" Gregory asked, as he removed his towel, stretched out face down while his masseuse got to work.

"Yes, I've got box seats. You bringing anyone?"

"Alondra Martin just cornered me for dinner, so I invited her. We'll do dinner at five. You want to come with?"

"Can't. My younger brother, Raymond, who we call Ray Ray, is in town. He got a two-day suspension for his foul language to another student."

"Bummer."

"Yeah, tell me. I'm having dinner at home with him and my uncle who is a former NYC cop. We need to see whether we can talk some sense into the knucklehead."

"I didn't know you had a sib."

"Two brothers. Elias is older than me by several years. He's in the Merchant Marines and Ray Ray is in junior high school in Mitchell County, Maryland. What about you?"

"I'm number four of five; two brothers both older. Kenneth James owns CompuCorrect in San Francisco and Santa Barbara. He's married to a foxx, JeNelle, junior US Senator for California and owner of

INSIGHTS, an art gallery, bookstore, and novelty emporium. They have four boys, two sets of twins and twin daughters."

"I've read about a Kenneth Alexander, former two-term California Governor and his business in *Entrepreneurs' Magazine* top one hundred. It's one of the fastest growing telecommunications companies in the country. I didn't make the connection."

"Yeah," Gregory grinned, "I saw the article. Then there's my brother, Benny, Colonel Benjamin Staton Alexander, US Air Force pilot; married to another smokin' hot, stone foxx, Stacy Greene, US Navy officer, both stationed in Tokyo, Japan, with four daughters and three sons."

"He is also designated to be the command pilot for the SPACEHOME program, isn't he? He's an astronaut."

"He is, yes. He's flown two missions, but he's scheduled to take another one. You really keep up. Two sisters, Vivian, older than me, is a US Appellate Court Judge who's married to Chuck Montgomery."

"Chucky P? The famous ball player?"

"Yes. As you probably remember, he gave up pro basketball years ago and is an Emergency Room medical doctor now. He and my sister have a houseful of natural born and adopted children. They adopt abandoned children with health challenges and live on a farm in Maryland outside of DC."

"Whoa! Wait! I read about a young woman, Vivian Alexander, a former Gold Medalist, who was married to Derrick 'Dunk and Jam' Jackson. He and Chucky P were tight back in the day. Years after DJ Jackson died, she married Chucky P. Talk about a foxx, the woman was Grade A Prime from the pictures I remember seeing of her. She reminds me of the actress Jada Pinkett-Smith. She's your sister?"

"Yeah."

"Man, as I recall, DJ Jackson was one of the youngest multi-billionaires at thirty-seven years old when he died. He created some type of medical software used to help identify diseases and other medical problems and made a mint. He owned Adventurer Executive Airline, (AEA), an island near Bimini, a ski resort, a medical practice, a string of yachts, all kinds of global investments and businesses. He had one helluva portfolio and your sister was what twenty-three when he died?"

"All true, but she was twenty-four. When they married, she'd already graduated from law school and passed the bar exam. The first year after their wedding they adopted several children from an orphanage where Derrick had a number of patients and Vivian was pregnant with their son at the time. Their boy, DJ Junior, was born on the day Derrick died. In fact Derrick was holding DJ in the hospital nursery when he had a heart attack. It was Chuck who found him in the hospital nursery and tried to revive him."

"Man, that's hard. You said there is one more sister?"

"Yes, Aretha Grace who is younger than me. She's at Harvard getting her masters and preparing to go to England to study at either Cambridge or Oxford, I forget which, for her doctorate."

"Your parents still around?"

"Dr. Bernard and Sylvia Benson Alexander are alive and well. Dad's an educator by profession who is now the state senator representing our home district in Summer County, South Carolina, to the state government in Columbia. Mom is the head of nursing at Summer County General Hospital and the head of the nursing school academy."

"You had a good childhood, I'll bet."

"The best. I couldn't help it. I have uncles, aunts, cousins on both the Alexander and Benson sides of the family up the ying yang. We are legion, but a very close-knit family unit," he said, laughing.

"You and Alondra looking to add to the size of your family?"

"Uh, that's a no. Just platonic friends. What about you and the stage actress, Yvonne Kincaid. She's starring in the play tonight, right?"

"Strictly social and yes, she's an accomplished actress. However, remind me to tell you about the one who got away sometime. She's married now, but she's the prototype for my ideal woman; the kind that's still on my radar. So I'm still looking."

"I know the feeling well. It's tradition in my family we only bring home to Summer County the person we intend to marry. Needless to say, I'm not booking any extra seats for flights home anytime soon."

They laughed as men would want to do about being confirmed bachelors.

"On a different note, I've been giving your partnership offer some thought," said Jackson. "I like what I see you and the others accomplishing with your full-service approach and personalized service. Your firm is out there on the cutting edge of discount brokerage, margin loans, and real estate investment. I read you're also looking to add an insurance arm to your operation as a full partner. You also have resources in specialty areas I need. For example, I haven't worked in the area of pension fund management the way you have. I've been strictly a portfolio manager. So, I'd like to be a part of your firm. If the offer is still on the table, I'd like to buy in."

"Your check in hand, your signature on the partnership agreement, and you can stick a fork in it and consider it done. Welcome aboard," Gregory said, with a fist bump while their masseuses continued to give them deep-muscle, hydro massages. When finished, the masseuses began the full-body scrub.

"Then, when we finish up here, let's head to your office and make the announcement."

Later that afternoon, when Alondra Martin entered through the glass doors of the CTI offices, she noticed workmen affixing a new name to the list of partners across the marble reception wall. The remnants of what looked like a party were being cleared away.

"Good afternoon, Ms. Martin," one of the three super-efficient male receptionists announced.

"Good afternoon. What's going on?" she asked, nodding toward the workmen.

"A new partner came on board today. We've been celebrating Jackson Chase's decision to join our firm. I'll let Mr. Alexander know you're here."

Though she didn't let her annoyance show, she was definitely angry. Gregory was a great guy and certainly arm candy, but she had been dating him for the last four months with the expectation, through him, she would be offered an opportunity to join CTI as an equity partner. The company was one of the fastest growing and most prestigious in the financial industry. Okay, so she recognized her credentials weren't as impressive or as strong as the founding partners. She barely made it out of undergrad and didn't finish grad school because of the chance to play basketball professionally overseas and later on an Arizona team. Unfortunately, she wasn't picked up for the third season with the Arizona team. She was essentially a one-trick pony. As an offensive player, she could run the real estate and score, but her defensive game was for shit. Teams wanted horses that could play both ends of the court. When her agent couldn't get her placed with another team, she was nearly flat broke. Her uncle got her a job in New York City at a bank where he was the General Manager. She was now Vice President of New Accounts; not particularly earth shattering among a bunch of mid-level managers with more important responsibilities, but still she was reaching for the brass ring: a seat on the New York Stock Exchange. Gregory Alexander was the express lane to that goal.

"Earth to Alondra," Gregory was saying.

She had been so embedded in her thoughts she blocked everything out except the workmen installing the name of a new partner on the wall where she wanted her name to be.

"Sorry," she said, tamping down her distraction, giving him what she hoped was a luminous smile. She would have to work harder on Gregory in order for him to offer her a place at his firm.

"You look great," he said, but thought, although she was certainly well put together for an evening on the town, there seemed to be something unpleasant in her eyes for just a moment and then it was gone.

Outside, on the street, they chatted in the private, hired town car on the way to the restaurant. When they arrived, a valet opened the car door and Gregory got out amid a crowd of cheering fans and others on a rope line. He reached back in to offer his hand to Alondra. He was used to camera flashes going off in his face nearly blinding him and rope lines where he gained access without having to wait. She stalled to pose for pictures before they were ushered inside where a maître d' quickly and efficiently handed them over to a waiter who led them to a VIP section.

The restaurant was obviously new and chic having a style that immediately welcomed you in to relax and enjoy. He liked the ambiance. The ambient lighting was perfect and the live music filtering in from a bar, The Run Way, and dance floor in another part of the building didn't overlay or prevent the flow of conversation at a normal volume. Nearly every table was filled and others came in after he and Alondra were seated.

At precisely five o'clock, to the sound of melodic strings and harp, gauzy tents with hooped skirts descended from the high ceiling surrounding the individual tables and the lighting lowered. The atmosphere gave an illusion of privacy in a sheltered garden setting to each table through the thin fabric. People could be seen, but mostly only in silhouette. A three-tiered candle arrangement burned in the center of the gaily-decorated, round table. Somewhere it seemed off in the distance, a waterfall tinkled and a brook soothingly bubbled.

Gregory appreciated the generously-sized, high-back chairs, with padded arm rests which didn't make his six-foot, ten-inch, two-hundred-thirty-pound body feel cramped and uncomfortable.

It intrigued him there was no menu. Apparently, everyone had whatever the chef decided to serve that day from soup to nuts. No substitutions. It was a part of the intrigue and ambiance along with the warm, peppermint-scented, hand towels distributed and removed before three wines were served. There was an awesome array of stemware and gleaming flatware already on the table in ridged formation and precise order. A basket held a generous grouping of small loaves of fresh, warm breads with flavored butters, cheeses, jams and seasoned oils. It was a delightful surprise to see what was coming next throughout the delicious seven course meal. Though the portions were not overly large, they were extremely filling and each dish was beautifully presented and complemented by a different wine.

Wait-staff served and cleared after each course as efficiently and as unobtrusively as brain surgeons ply their trade. At the end of the meal, over an exceptional coffee and aperitif, Gregory declared the food lived up to the incredible ambiance. He paid the tab without paying close attention to the bill and added a generous tip.

A smattering of applause started and grew in intensity as the tents rose to the ceiling again and the lights grew brighter. People began to stand as a spotlight focused on a vision of absolute loveliness who appeared near the exit. With his superior height, Gregory's eyes latched on to someone he hadn't seen in far too long.

Angelique Teresa Menendez-Gaza.

Her guests were always so gracious in their compliments, thought Angelique. Word of mouth had rapidly spread and her restaurant, Angelique's Place, was trending up toward the top fifty in the city. recent movie shot food and restaurant critics predicted she would be in the top twenty-five before the end of her first year of operation. She was pleased though she had to stick to a grueling schedule to ensure the quality of the food and the service remained top notch. She wished her bottom line reflected the success the critics predicted. She sat two hundred give or take at each seating. There were three seatings per night. The early seating was timed to serve the pre-theatre crowd; then the evening diners, a more laid back European-Continental crowd; and then the post-theatre crowd who were heading out the door by midnight. If she were really lucky, she could be in her bed and asleep by one in the morning. By eight, she was up and out at the commercial restaurant markets with her other specialty chefs deciding on what to buy to enhance that night's menu.

Presentation was another key element of her unique service. Fresh flowers were ordered daily and given away to anyone of her customers celebrating a special occasion. A flower was also pinned to the lapel of each parting guest. It was a signature Angelique's Place affectation which never failed to garner great advertising for the restaurant. Patrons were often asked where the flower came from because of its unusual beauty. Actually, the flower was unique to Peru, but cultivated in the US by a hydroponics farm, Alexander-Dixon Industries in Summer County, South Carolina, and delivered along with freshly canned fruits and vegetables which were part of the secret of her successful menus. They bought much of their meat, poultry, and fish from the same source, and then added other delicacies from local wholesale markets.

Her thoughts were partially on the Friday menu and what fish she would serve and partially on the woman, who was renewing old acquaintances with her. She was one of the fashion buyers from McCoy's, a huge, upscale, boutique department store similar to Neiman-Marcus, who wanted Angelique to be a judge at a fashion show of new designers for teen clothing. Over the woman's head, Angelique spotted her one-time heartthrob, Gregory Clayton Alexander. Even after all the intervening years, her heart had a rampageous reaction to his mere presence. She hadn't seen or talked with him in quite a while, but he hadn't changed except he was even more handsome than before. His face may have changed from a youthful boy to a man with a short beard and mustache, but it only enhanced his magazine-cover good looks. She wanted to swoon at the way his tall, well-built body filled out his custom-made designer suit. He was perfection personified.

"Angelique? Angelique? Are you still with me, dear?" the McCoy's buyer continued.

"Yes, uh, yes, Brittany. I'll give your request some consideration and speak with my agent," she said, distractedly accepting the woman's business card. She would have agreed to eat ground glass in order to move the woman along and get to Gregory, but she knew better than to commit to any public appearance without Bill Chandler's expressed direction.

As Gregory was next in line, she noted with no little amount of disappointment he was not alone. Nevertheless, she pumped up the wattage of her smile and accepted his hand.

"Angel Face," Gregory said, calling her by his pet childhood nickname for her, his face wreathed in a matinee-idol smile. "I didn't know you were in the city."

"Yes, a little less than six months now."

"Hello, I'm Alondra Martin. You two know each other?"

"Well, I guess you could say that," Angelique said, cautiously.

"My apology, Alondra. Yes, Angelique and I practically grew up together," said Gregory who had yet to release her hand. "She and my sister, Aretha Grace, are best friends."

She chuckled, but there was a damnable electric spark charging through her system just from looking into his mesmerizing eyes and holding his hand. It had always been like that no matter how innocently he touched her. He treated her just as he did his kid sister, Aretha, her BFF, except for one precious moment when he danced with her at her Sweet Sixteen birthday party and kissed her on her mouth.

Alondra must have noticed what felt like chemistry sparking between them, thought Gregory because she possessively claimed his arm causing him to release Angelique's hand.

"Nice to meet you, Angelique. Your restaurant is wonderful. We'll be back, I'm sure, won't we, Gregory? For now we have to go, if we're going to be seated before the curtain goes up."

"Yes, all right," he said, reluctantly, but he really wanted to stay and visit with his young friend. "It's good to see you, Angel."

"Thank you for coming," she said, forcing herself to turn away and greet the next person in line.

Gregory watched Angelique as one of the wait-staff pinned a flower on Alondra's wrap and his lapel, before they hurried out the door to the waiting car service.

"So you grew up with the world famous model Angelique?" Alondra asked, once seated in the car.

"As I said, she's my younger sister's best friend. She was just a kid when I knew her."

"Well, she certainly isn't a kid anymore."

Truer words, thought Gregory. Angelique was always a looker with those dark, expressive eyes and creamy complexion lightly tinged with brown, red and golden undertones, with raven-wing eyebrows and long, thick lashes. Her cheek bones were high and she had a delectable wide mobile mouth with pillow-soft looking lips. Her hair was long to midway her back and glossy like liquid asphalt that naturally waved and curled. She was a favorite spokesperson for a popular hair-care manufacturer and did public service announcements for several youth-related causes. She was tall for her age back in the day, all arms and legs that went on forever. She grew into her body and filled out nicely from the days when she used to come to visit him on UVAs campus during sports' events with his sister, Aretha, and their friends, Margo Chandler and Joyce Montgomery. Angelique was the youngest in the group of female friends.

He remembered seeing her on magazine covers at airports and other newsstands or seeing her in television commercials or daytime or late night talk shows from time to time. The press and news media often caught shots of her on the arm of some notable celebrity. He hadn't seen her most recent movie shot last year, but he had them all in his collection. She spent a lot of time in Europe, he recalled Aretha saying after she visited Angelique in Paris, but he lost touch after he left college and began his professional career.

"Are the rumors about Angelique and a certain prince of the British realm true?"

"I wouldn't know. I don't follow gossip and I don't carry it."

"I remember reading about her after her brother won the Academy Award for best supporting actor. He was, what, about nine years old at the time?"

"Actually, as I remember he was eight."

"You must know him too, then."

"I do, yes, though, like Angel, I haven't seen him in person in years. He's in college now. We share an agent and I understand Miguel's schedule, with modeling and acting commitments, is jam packed. A movie he shot in Italy earlier this year is being released this fall."

The car pulled to the curb in front of the theatre and the driver got out opening the door for them. Just as they stepped onto the curb, Jackson Chase was getting out of the car ahead of them. They joined up amid a flashing photography lights to go into the theatre lobby on the red carpet. From the lobby to their box seats, Alondra forced them to pose again for photographers and chatted Jackson up about Angelique's until the lights lowered and the curtain came up.

The show, a Revival of the 1865-1880 Dan Lewis *"Cant Dem Melon Down"* and Sam Lucas and the Hyers Sisters collection: *Every Day'l Be Sunday By and By; Good-bye, Old Cabin Home; Oh, I'll Meet You Dar; and Since I Saw de Cotton Grow*, was performed in the dialect and vernacular of the old South. His Aunt Mariah told him about Anna Madah and Emma Louise Hyers, singers and pioneers of black musical theater, who produced the first full-fledged musical plays, including *Out of Bondage* which premiered in 1876. It reminded Gregory of the stories his family's elders told about his ancestors who were performers and composers touring in Europe and North Africa with the great Josephine Baker until the war chased them home. His Aunt Mariah, one of his mother's older sisters, the renowned actress and songstress, the French Mariah, was still living in Paris, France. She performed regularly at her very popular restaurant and club, Mariah's. He'd be sure to call her and let her know the Hyers sisters' legacy was being presented to a new generation nearly a hundred forty years later. She'd get a real kick out of that. Now that he had more control over his time, he would arrange to visit her in Paris in the spring.

Yvonne Kincaid was a sensational talent and received a standing ovation and several curtain calls. Jackson had backstage passes so they went to Yvonne's dressing room, but only stayed a short time.

When he and Alondra got into the town car again, she kissed him and whispered "Your place or mine?" That surprised him. Their relationship was strictly platonic up until that point. He had made no overt moves to introduce sex into the equation.

Since, as a rule, he didn't take women to his place, he opted to go to hers. Before they got naked, he made it clear he wasn't in the market for an exclusive, full-time, long-term relationship. She said she was in agreement with that position. He spent the night, but for some reason though his body was geared to meet her needs, his mind wasn't in it. He kept thinking about Angelique. As a result, he left early the next morning before breakfast.

<hr />

After seeing Gregory, Angelique was in no hurry to return to her condo above the restaurant, so she sat in the kitchen and had a light snack while her friend, Maxwell Kennard, III, Trey to his friends, had a hardy meal at her staff table. The kitchen crew was cleaning up and storing what was left in containers for delivery to the homeless shelter nearest to her restaurant. Kitchen debris was put into a compost machine that made short work of the results. The compost was bagged and used by her staff in community gardens in and around the city. No scraps were wasted. Even the bones were saved and given to animal shelters.

"What's on your mind, Angel?" asked Trey. "You've been in a daze since you sat down," he said, wiping his hands and mouth with a napkin.

She looked up at the handsome man with startlingly beautiful green eyes. Folding her arms on the table, she asked, "Why haven't you hit on me, Trey?"

He smirked at her, leaning back comfortably in his chair. "Believe me, Angel, it's not because the thought hasn't crossed my mind, but my intimate relationships tend to be short-termed. I want to keep your friendship because no matter when I show up, you feed me great food."

Trey, a musical genius, was a producer, director, and showman. He scored music for award-winning movies and theatrical events, like the Oscars. Devilishly handsome, he had a kind of laid-back charisma that had women salivating.

"Is it only my friendship and food holding you back?"

"Uh, where is this conversation going, babe?" he asked, taking a sip of his wine.

"I'm in love, Trey, but he isn't in love with me. I don't have any defenses where he's concerned, but he obviously has many when it concerns me. I just wondered whether I'm just not appealing to some men. He's about your age and popular with the ladies the way you are, so I'm just curious."

"*Whew!*" he said, demonstratively. "I thought I was going to have to make love to you to keep our friendship."

She laughed at his antics. "Come on, Trey, tell me," she entreated. "What's wrong with me?"

"From my perspective, not a thing. You're beautiful and you're an excellent chef. You've heard that the way to a man's heart is through his stomach. Cook for him and he'll be yours forever."

She gave him a sardonic look.

"However," he continued, "for some men, we have to be open to a serious, long-term, intimate relationship. My green light isn't on where you're concerned. It's not you, Angelique, it's me. I can't image most men don't find you stunningly attractive. Still, you've got plenty of time to find the right match for you."

"Plenty of time because I'm young," she said and sighed.

"Well, yeah, I suppose. Some men go for jail bait," he teased.

She pursed her lips and threw her napkin at him. "I'll be twenty-one this year, I'll have you know. I'm not jail bait."

"I'm about ten years your senior, but we don't speak the same language. We're almost a whole half a generation apart. We don't speak the same language."

"Could that be a big impediment for some men?"

"Yes, babe, it could. Some men prefer women with a little more experience."

She thought about that for a moment. Could it be that it wasn't so much the differences in her age and Gregory's but their life experiences? She looked up as Trey rose from his seat. "You're leaving already?" she asked.

"Oh, yeah. You're too much of a temptation for me. Besides, it's after midnight and your kitchen helpers have finished cleaning. Come on,

I'll ride up in the elevator with you. However, that's as far as I'm going because I want to maintain our friendship."

She laughed and snaked her arm through his. "I could work miracles in the elevator."

"That's what I'm afraid of, jail bait."

Chapter 2

"So what's the trading platform," Gregory asked Jackson a few weeks later. They were in the executive break room of the CTI business offices across the street from the Stock Exchange.

"For now, full-service banking, investments, and financial products. I don't envision anything more complex than that at the moment. Certainly not the purchase or sale of securities. I've been financing a few businesses in Harlem and in my old neighborhood in Mitchell County, Maryland, under the trade name MC Financial."

"So you're going to make MC Financial an arm of your new, Maryland state-chartered bank?"

"For now, I'll keep them separate, and make it an independent investment bank."

"Do you want Compliant to underwrite?"

"I have enough in my current portfolio to do it on my own for now."

"I should say. You made a killing in the market last week," Gregory said, laughing. "They're calling you the Wizard of Wall Street. I'm glad you agreed to come on board."

"I need the type of large cap brokerage this firm offers. It takes the weight off of my shoulders not to have to do it all as a one-man operation. For me, it's a win-win situation."

"You bring a lot to the table too, Jackson. Your private equity fund clients and private placement business get a large number of small investors in the door. We can expand on this with the discount online brokerage clients. That allows us to aggregate orders from a large number of small investors. With Adam adding the insurance arm to Compliant, we're getting a substantial number of colleges and universities investing in mutual funds, the private equity market, and hedge funds."

"I feel comfortable putting this business in the hands of Compliant's junior partners and agents while I tackle establishing the bank in Maryland."

"We live in a virtual-reality world, Jackson. You're a Skype away. If you need help, just holla."

"I'll keep it in mind, but I'll be here for more than a year while I get the infrastructure built and operational. I purchased land in the middle of town including a car dealership and an old, closed, movie theatre. I'm using the square footage and other vacant land to build a three-level, enclosed shopping mall and parking facility around the bank. So I'm not folding my tent quite yet to move back to Mitchell County. I'll keep my place in Harlem and in The Hamptons for now. It doesn't make sense to sell in this down market."

"You're right about that."

"Right about what?" China McAllister, CTI's managing partner, asked, as she came into the breakroom for a cup of coffee. A more gorgeous woman Gregory and Jackson had never seen, but they were used to her startling blue eyes, the hint of coffee in her creamy skin tone, and her body a chiseled perfection.

"Jackson was filling me in on the bank and enclosed shopping mall he's building in Mitchell County, Maryland."

"Oh, yes, I've tried to get him to let me buy a piece of it, but he's not willing to let me in . . . yet, but I'm wearing him down. He's going the sole-proprietorship route. When he mentioned it to me, I did a little research. Mitchell County is prime. It's located between Annapolis and Baltimore, Maryland, and within spitting distance of Washington, DC. There's a lot of money in that triangle and Jackson is going to be pretty much the only game in town."

Jackson laughed at her peak. "I'm talking with Justin McCoy about putting in one of his resort hotels and conference centers. There's nothing of that caliber anywhere near Mitchell County. The old guard has pretty much kept development low and the wages stagnant. I was born and grew up on the wrong side of the tracks there so I know the lay of the political landscape. The county needs some new blood or it's going to lose all of its young people to other counties or to bigger cities. The fishing industry is slowly coming back, especially after the oil spill in the Gulf. People still don't trust the sea catch from around there. Land is still relatively inexpensive, and the tax base is low. I have my eye on a tract of waterfront land along the Chesapeake Bay. It's prime for a low-density, estate-sized housing development. The area is also perfect for tourism, boating, and fishing. It could become another Nantucket especially along the city docks and beach-front Chesapeake Bay. The county's got a good base for cottage industries. It only has a few five-star restaurants and an aging country club. It just needs a shove in the right direction. Mitchell County Bank and Trust (MCB&T) will help smooth out the landscape."

"See, that's why we brought you on board," Gregory said, and slapped Jackson on his back, but the mention of a restaurant put him in mind of Angelique's Place. He had been thinking about her a lot over the intervening weeks.

After he got his coffee, he left Jackson and China chatting in the breakroom and started toward his office. When he passed Joyce Montgomery's office, another of Angelique's close friends, he noticed her Executive Assistant was away from her desk and Joyce's door was open. He stepped into the door frame with the intention of asking her about Angelique and observed she had three computer screens on her desk, one always tuned to stock market reports from different countries constantly moving across the screen. How she read information in different languages was a wonder to him. Still, she was swift. She was a CPA with a doctorate and a wiz on CTI's accounts and portfolios. She constantly updated data, adjusting their standing, and answering margin calls from agents on the floor of the Exchange across the street.

"Did you see the new options that became available today for the International Forest Company?" she spontaneously asked, without otherwise telegraphing prior acknowledgement of his presence. "That's a BlackHawk Global property."

"It is, yes. I saw it on the Stock Options Channel. I put in a call to Roderick and JaiHonnah Baylor earlier. They're still managing BlackHawk's portfolio while JaiHonnah's father is an American ambassador in Africa. The strike price represents an approximate two percent discount to the current trading price. It is also possible the put contract would expire worthless."

"Yeah, I saw it. The analytical data I've gathered suggests the current odds of it happening are sixty-six percent."

"I'm still going to track those odds over time to see how they change. I don't want to put our clients in the market prematurely, but sometimes it's the type of long shot that could pay off big. I'm going to develop a high-risk portfolio and put it on our website. I'll see who out there wants a challenge."

She clicked her mouse on a twelve-month history chart. Then she picked up her phone on half a ring. "Buy as much as you can get of GTE when it reaches forty dollars a share," she said, and hung up. Shortly, her buy call appeared on the reader board and simultaneously set off a frantic flurry of activity on the trading floor. She sat back and laced her fingers behind her head. "Talk with Peter lately?"

"Last month sometime," Gregory answered, cautiously. Peter Callaway was Gregory's friend and former housemate from his college days. He was an engineering student from Tennessee who played football with more heart than talent. Gregory introduced Peter to Joyce during her first year at American University and, since they were both born and raised on farms, they immediately hit it off. They were still as tight as twins in a womb, but at a distance. Peter lived in landlocked Tennessee all of his life and never saw an ocean. One summer during their sophomore year, Gregory took Peter to his great grandaunt's oceanfront home on South Carolina's Grand Strand. Once Peter saw the Atlantic Ocean for the first time, he was hooked. Since then Peter had traveled to the five principal salt water oceans around the globe picking up engineering jobs along the way.

"Your pal and the love of my life has signed on to crew a sail boat in a regatta for a French company. Initially, he was supposed to be designing new riggings and sails for the yacht races only for a few months. Now he's planning to be in Australia for a few years."

Gregory was surprised and, in a way, felt responsible for Peter's love of all things related to the deep blue. "Maybe you should take some time to go visit him."

"If I'm not enough for him to want to come home, settle down, and marry me, then maybe I'm not the one for him."

"You don't have a 'use by' date stamped on your forehead, Joyce. Maybe he just needs a little more time to spread his sails on the sea and live his dream."

"I want whatever he wants that will make him happy, but I also want him to feel the same way about me. That's not happening. He's trading a life with me for a yacht race. Hell, I live on friggin' Manhattan Island. If all he wanted to do was sail, I'd buy a boat for him and he could sail around this island all day long." She huffed a frustrated breath and then shook her head as if to clear it. "Oh, hell, Greg, I didn't mean to unload on you. It's just that I'm in love with that big Tennessee galoot. I want to marry him and have babies with him; spend the rest of our lives loving each other, but it doesn't look like any of that's going to happen."

He wanted to say he was sorry. After all, he was the reason they met all those years ago in college and why Peter took to the sea, but he also knew what it meant to follow his dreams and fulfill a life quest.

"Speaking of old times, I had lunch with Angelique the other day. She said you were in her restaurant a few weeks ago, but she hadn't heard from you since."

"I was, yes. I went with Alondra Martin."

When Joyce wrinkled her nose, Gregory chuckled. He knew Joyce didn't care for Alondra and the feeling was mutual. They had a kind of city girl v. country girl rivalry going on. Joyce Montgomery was born and raised on a farm in Monroe County, Pennsylvania, with her brother Chuck and their eleven other siblings. Alondra came up on the mean streets of Detroit, Michigan, in a large family, too. Alondra considered Joyce a hick country bumpkin and Joyce considered Alondra a ghetto queen and never the twain shall meet.

"Do you want to go to dinner tonight at Angelique's? I could probably get reservations."

"I can't tonight. I've agreed to be Alondra's plus one for some black-tie function her bank is holding."

"She's certainly getting a lot of mileage out of having you on her arm. I've seen your mug in the society blogs several times."

He laughed, but he and Alondra were seeing quite a bit of each other three to four times a week in addition to playing on opposing basketball teams. Though the sex was good, not great, but good, he didn't want it to become habit forming. Plus, he had been thinking about Angelique quite a bit. He called his sister specifically to talk about her. Aretha always kept up with everyone's news and activities. Her family blog was both thorough and hilarious. She already knew he and Alondra were in the restaurant and was surprised he didn't know Angelique had opened her restaurant earlier in the year.

He said a few parting words to Joyce before continuing to his office. His Executive Assistant had a number of hot items on his agenda keeping him grounded for the rest of the day. Still, he managed to get a message through to his pal Peter. When he met with Alondra at her bank's annual awards banquet, a number of her coworkers and bosses cornered him for stock tips. That happened a lot when he was out and about. Either someone wanted to rehash some game he played an eon ago in college or in the NBA against a favorite team or talk shop. After a long day from seven in the morning to nearly seven at night he wasn't in the mood to use the event as a networking opportunity. So for those who button-holed him for his time and attention, he handed out his business card and suggested they call his office for an appointment.

That evening, he begged off spending the night with Alondra and, after dropping her at her home, directed the car service driver to take him home. By chance, while heading home, the driver passed Angelique's just as the late night diners let out a little after midnight. He was stuck in the heavy flow of traffic for more than fifteen minutes before he decided to get out of the car in front of the restaurant. As the doorman was closing up for the night, Gregory approached.

"Good evening, sir. Is Ms. Menendez-Gaza still here?"

"Certainly, yes, sir, she is," he said, stepping aside to let him enter and then closing and locking the door behind them. "This way, Mr. Alexander."

It still amazed Gregory when perfect strangers recognized him on sight. His height alone generally caused some people to stop and stare, but not always with name recognition. "Thank you, Mr. ...?" he questioned, extending his hand.

"Conway, Roy Conway," he said, and firmly shook the older man's hand, his face breaking into a broad smile.

"Thank you, Mr. Conway," he said. "You're a military man, aren't you?"

The man's smile broadened. "I am, yes. A Marine. How did you know?"

"My brother is an Air Force jet fighter pilot. It's just something about the military comportment that's unmistakable. Thank you for your service."

"You're welcome."

He was led into the restaurant side of the building, but he could see through the etched-glass partition panels the bar, the Run Way, and dance floor were still jam packed. Someone was crooning into the microphone and playing a piano while patrons danced cheek-to-cheek.

Angelique sat at one of the tables in the deserted restaurant with bits and pieces of paper spread out in front of her and adding figures on a pad of paper. In a show of obvious frustration, she spread her fingers in her hair as if she would tear the long, silky strands from her scalp. Her back was toward them when they entered. As they approached she let out what had to be an imaginative string of invectives in Spanish. She muttered so rapidly Gregory only caught a few words.

"Ms. Angelique?" Mr. Conway interrupted.

"Yes, Roy?" she asked, distractedly.

"Someone to see you, miss."

"It's not Mr. Durant again, is it?"

"No, miss, not this time, though I refused him entrance earlier tonight."

"Then who . . .?" she asked, as she turned around in her seat.

She looked tired until she saw him. Gregory delighted in the way her face brightened and her million-dollar smile lit the room.

"Greg," she said, springing up and rushing to greet him.

She went easily into his arms. He was immediately taken back so many years ago when she was still a gangly teen at her Sweet Sixteen party. As they danced he remembered how she looked up at him with what he rationalized was youthful infatuation. After all, she was just a kid while he was nearly in his mid-twenties. Yet, the light shining in her luminous eyes was lethal to his senses. In a moment of pure insanity she went up on her toes and met her mouth to his in a brief, but disconcerting kiss. For long ponderous weeks, months, even years afterward she was embedded in his thoughts to the point of instantaneous heat suffusing his body and wreaking havoc with his libido anytime he thought of her, much the same way he felt now.

He set her away from him at arms' length before she could feel the effect she had on his body, but felt compelled to keep his hands on her. "How are you, Angel Face?"

"I'm fine, but I truly miss hearing you call me that silly name. It's been years."

"It has, yes. I'm sorry for it. Recently I've been putting together a new venture."

"Yes, I know, with Joyce and Margo. Come, please sit, and tell me all about it."

"You don't want to hear about it at this time of night."

"Of course I do, but first what can I get for you? Something to eat or to drink?"

"Really, I'm fine. Don't bother."

"It's no bother. Wait here. Don't move a muscle," she said, as she hurried away.

Gregory looked so good, Angelique thought as she quickly moved around her workers in the kitchen putting together a snack tray. His tall, statuesque frame gave life to his black Italian *Haute Couture* tuxedo and white tailor-made shirt opened at the neck with onyx studs. His black Hermes bow tie was undone and hanging loosely around his neck. He could have easily been Hermes, the messenger of the gods of Greek mythology and the son of Zeus; the patron of athletes and trade. His Adventurer cologne smelled indescribably delicious on him. She knew quality when she saw it and he wore it well. After all it had been her stock and trade for many years.

A space just to the left of his chin pulsated with life. She wanted to lay her mouth there, just there to feel the pump of his heart under her lips. Closing her eyes for a moment, she took a deep, calming breath. It didn't matter how her staff looked askance at her before she hefted the silver tray lined with a pretty paper doily and an assortment of delectable delights. Her sommelier handed a bottle of their newly featured wine and two, chilled, stemmed glasses to her and then scurried ahead of her to open the door. Her hands were full, but so was her youthful heart when Gregory looked up, stood, and warmly smiled at her return.

She carried a tray of cheeses, breads, and fruits, including strawberries and white grapes, with miniature sandwiches and ice cold, white wine, water, and two fine crystal goblets. He sat again, after she was seated, looking at the beautifully appointed restaurant. He had not intended to snoop behind her back, but even reading upside down he noted she was struggling to balance her accounts and making little mistakes with simple bookkeeping entries in her daily expense sheet.

"I know you don't drink hard alcohol, but I also know you do like wine. I want you to try this one I'm thinking of featuring for the restaurant. Kenneth and JeNelle sent a case of it to me, and I like it," she said, as she poured a bit into a wine glass for him to sample.

He cut a piece of hard cheese to clear his palate before he tasted the wine. "Ah, this is from a Napa Valley vineyard; a vintner JeNelle knows and works with on the Business and Professional Women's League. Her name is . . ." he said, closing his eyes to bring the name to mind as he sniffed the bouquet. It was entirely too distracting trying to think and look at Angelique's beautiful, angelic face, and gather a whiff of her intoxicating scent, simultaneously, "Florence Ewing," he said, snapping his finger.

Angelique giggled, delighted, "You're right. You're exactly right. How did you know?"

"I received a case of the same assorted wines from Kenneth and JeNelle for the holidays," he said, as they shared the assortment of food on the tray.

"Then it was not selected just for me," she said, disappointment evident in her voice.

She bit into a fat, juicy, chocolate-covered strawberry and the image went straight to his loins.

"Very special," he said, just above a whisper, his breath backing up in his chest. "They only sent a case of wine to family members."

Her face immediately brightened. It pleased her tremendously to still be considered a member of the Alexander family. The only thing was she wanted desperately to be a family member through marriage to Gregory.

"So, I really like your restaurant. You've done an excellent job."

She looked around the empty dining room as if seeing it from his perspective. "I worked really hard to make it unique. I've traveled so much and eaten in some of the most fabulous places, so I had an idea of what I wanted, but I'm not sure how long it's going to last," she said, on a windy sigh. "I learned so much about cooking from *momi* and then I studied at Le Cordon Bleu between jobs."

"Why wouldn't it last? Did you make a mistake in your business plan?" At her blank stare, he asked, "You do have a business plan, don't you?"

She shrugged. "I really don't understand all the business about statistics, projections, and strategic management."

"Wait, what? You're not telling me Bill Chandler didn't work this entire plan out with you, are you? I know he is still your agent because he's my agent, too, but this doesn't sound like him."

"He wanted to, but I wouldn't let him. He's already done so much for me and my family since we came to America when I was eight years old. I just wanted to do something on my own without bothering him for his help."

"Okay, I understand, but why didn't you come to me, Joyce or Margo for help?"

"You were all so busy. What you do is so complicated. You deal with billions of dollars every day. I didn't want to bother anyone with this."

"Angel, this is what we do every day. We help people start businesses, expand, and find investors. We would have helped find investors for you or backed you ourselves. Your celebrity alone would have brought in millions."

"I don't have investors except Miguel."

Gregory just stared and then palmed his face dragging his right hand down his facial features to support his chin on his open fist with his elbow on the table. "Tomorrow is Saturday," he said, and then looked at his watch. "Correction. Today is Saturday. Our business offices are closed, so I want you to pack all of your papers and bring them to my home." He jotted his address and cell phone number on the pad before her. "Be prepared to spend a very intense day getting intimately involved with your business reorganization. So, plan not to be here tomorrow when your restaurant opens."

"Couldn't we work here? I mean I have an office."

"I mentor two boys on weekends and I coach a little league team. I need to be in my neighborhood. Now, can you make it?"

She shrugged. She really hadn't taken any time off since she opened. She could let her chef de cuisine take the lead for a day. Perhaps she'd be there before the last course was served. "What time?"

"I run at six-thirty in the morning, so make it about seven-thirty."

"Okay," she said, and sighed.

He checked his watch again. "If you're ready to shut down for the night, I'll take you home."

She giggled. "I live upstairs in this building. I can use the interior stairs or elevator to reach my flat or go out the front and go next door.

The doorman, Harry, will be snoozing, but he's a light sleeper. He'll let me in."

"Well, on that note, I'll say good night."

They embraced and, Mr. Conway, who also doubled as the night watchman, locked up behind him.

Chapter 3

Angelique wasn't sure she had the right address, but the car service driver assured her the address for the building that looked like a big fire department station house on a corner lot was, indeed, the one Gregory had written on her pad. She was a little early and eager to see Gregory again. So she tipped her driver when he opened her door, got out of the car, walked to the solid wood double doors, and rang the bell. Moments later one of the doors was opened by a tennis-shoe wearing older woman in a house dress with a rag tied around her full head of salt-and-pepper hair who was animatedly talking on a cell phone.

"Wait a minute, Mildred! Just hold your horses," she said into the phone, then huffed out her frustration before she turned to greet Angelique with a warm smile. "Yes, may I help you, dear?"

"Uh, is this Gregory Alexander's home?"

"You must be his Angel Face. You're certainly as pretty as he said you'd be. He's expecting you, but I don't think quite this early. It's not seven o'clock yet. Be that as it may, you come on in here out of the chill. He should be here in a moment. I had him stop at the bodega down the block to pick me up some of that pine cleaner and some other supplies on his way back," she said, while leading the way up unusually wide, open, thick, teakwood steps that seemed to float unsupported.

Though the woman never stopped talking, Angelique pretty much dialed her out when she got a look at the incredible amount of space. Her driver followed her into the wide vestibule carrying two stacked boxes. Through wide, but squat transom windows as they ascended the stairs, she got a glimpse of cars in the bays where emergency vehicles would have parked. As they reached the top of the first flight of stairs, a huge, completely open expanse of floor large enough to play full-court basketball, greeted her. There was a space allotted for essentially high-end, gourmet kitchen appliances and cabinets on exposed, lacquered, red brick walls; another space with four giant flat screens stacked two side-by-side with comfortable-looking, over-sized club chairs scattered around. Another area, the only one with a door, was tucked back under the floating stairs with the continuation of the thick, teakwood treads surrounded by books on shelves spanning so high a ladder ran on a track across the face. On the back side of the wall was another door to a large, modern powder room. The open stairs seemed to go up it appeared at least two more levels. The high ceilings held tiny pot lights, huge fans turning and circulating the air, and moving the leaves of the tree-sized plants statically placed throughout the expanse. The heated floor was a polished concrete with attractive, warm color variations. Periodically, thick Aubusson rugs under eye-catching oversized furniture defined conversation areas, but otherwise the immense space was devoid of clutter.

Huge high, wide, warehouse-sized windows surrounded the space on each wall and let in an incredible amount of natural light complementing the huge oil paintings she recognized as Russell Greene originals. The famous artist was Gregory's sister-in-law's younger brother. Also, Russell and Gregory's sister, Aretha, had been an item for many years. An area where a desk stood proud of a marble wall contained an array of family portraits in black and white. The shapes were all inconsistent, but fit together to make a nice wall-sized collage. There was an oblong, four-foot-long, two-foot-high photograph of his family members probably taken at their last Fourth of July family reunion in Summer County, South Carolina.

"So I was telling Mildred . . . . Oh, for Pete's sake. Mildred?" she barked, placing the phone to her ear again. "Are you there, Mildred? Well, I'll be! She calls me up before can't see in the morning to complain about that dang fool husband of hers and then she hangs up. Told that woman not to marry that old reprobate in the first dang place, but would she listen to me? Nooooo. Heck no! I was married to him for twenty-three years before he ran off with Maxine leaving me with his babies to raise and all, but nothing Mildred must do after he was with Maxine for thirteen years, but take him from her. Now they been married eleven years and he's out there chasin' behind another tail; probably our cousin Phyllis. She's the only one who hasn't had a taste of him yet. Well, at least I don't think she has. So what does she do but call me up, Mildred I mean, not Phyllis, complaining about him not coming home last night asking where he might be. As if I give a swift kitty about that man. He ain't never hit a lick at a snake or been worth nothing but to eat and make pretty babies. Now I reckon he's too old to make the babies, so what's he got left but that pretty face?"

Angelique had a feeling she shouldn't ask, but her curiosity got the better of her. "Your former husband's third wife called you looking for him?"

"Well, now, she's actually his fourth wife and my second cousin on momma's side, but so is Maxine on my daddy's side. He married another first cousin, June, before he married me. You see they was only sixteen when they got married and then had two quick babies, but it only lasted five years. They all had a hankering for my Melvin, but so did I back in the day. He's a pretty man with real good hair and all the right moves . . . if you know what I mean. Didn't need to call the plumber 'cause that man could lay down some pipe mornin', noon, and night," she said, with a school-girl giggle. "I raised up his other two kids, both girls, married now with families of their own, but he made my Sammy in his image. Heaven knows he's just like his daddy off running after some woman down there in Barbados where we was all born from originally. Ain't been back to see . . . oh, for heaven sake, where is my head this morning? That dang fool woman's got me all turned around. Sit yourself down anywhere and put those boxes over on the trestle table by the desk. You want something to eat or drink? I'm going to fix some food as soon as those boys get back."

"No, thank you, Mrs. . . . ?"

"Joyner. Janie Joyner."

"Your cousin's name is June?"

"Yes, siree. We was thick as thieves when we was brought up together. When you saw one of us it was always with the other. June and Janie, we are like Frick and Frack."

Her curiosity sated, she moved on. "Mrs. Joyner, you said Gregory would be back...?" she asked, as she acknowledged with a nod the driver's amused expression and tip of the hat at his departure.

"Of course. He went out for his regular run and took my grand boys with him. That boy, that Gregory, is a pure blessing. Saw me sittin' out on the street after my grand boys' no good mother stole my rent money and I lost my job at the hospital because of cut backs. Well, sir, I never been down so low and I didn't know what to do, but here he comes up the street on his way walking home from work as big and handsome as you please. I seen him before and he was always nice and spoke to me and my grands when he passed by. This time he stops and asks what happened. I tells him the Super put me and my grand boys out on the street 'cause I couldn't pay the rent. It wasn't nothing but a roach motel in the first place, but it was all I could afford at the time.

"Well, sir, the next thing I know, Gregory, he gets on his little phone and calls one of them PODs people to come and we load everything into the storage except our clothes and shoes, and my things get carted away. He brings everything else here into the garage to get the bugs out. Then he takes us to the Laundromat round the corner to wash and dry clean the clothes to make sure everything in our things is dead. He has us stay here with him while he buys the old, run-down, roach motel and the building next to it. He brings this architect and engineer, Ms. JaiHonnah and her husband, the fine basketball player, Mr. JRock who owns a construction company in DC, to renovate them old places into nice, big apartments with no rats or roaches. Then he goes and makes me the Super. Now I got me a job where I can be home all day and a big, rent free, three-bedroom, two bath apartment for me and my grand boys. You can't find this kinda space nowhere in this city for what I used to earn. All I have to pay for are my telephone, internet and cable TV service outta what I make as the Super. I can't thank the boy enough for what he done and he treats me like a queen so I come here every Saturday to clean for him while he's out running. Can you image he still wants to pay me for it? I won't take a penny from him, no sir! I got me some nice, respectable business peoples living in the building and they pays on time every month. I pay all the bills and I keep the building spic and span. Some of them tenants ask me to clean or cook for them on a regular. Now I got me one of those money-market savings accounts for my grand boys to help them go to college or trade school. Gregory, he set all of it up."

Just then the front door opened and, to Angelique's ears, it sounded like a herd of buffalo were galloping up the stairs. Gregory's face was the first one she saw breach the top of the landing and then two, tall, sandy-haired boys of about eleven and thirteen came running up the steps beside him.

"Whoa! Man, get that!" one exclaimed.

"That's no way to address a lady, Dejon. You and Keaton know what you're supposed to do," Gregory pointedly said.

The boys huffed, slouched, and rolled their eyes, but they both walked to Angelique and one at a time, extended a hand.

"Hi, my name is Dejon Joyner."

"Hi, my name is Keaton Joyner."

"It's nice to meet two such handsome and mannerly young men. My name is Angelique Teresa Menendez-Gaza."

"You Puerto Rican?" Dejon asked.

"Peruvian originally."

"Whatever! You're still a foxx! Is that your real hair or—"

"Enough. Here, take these bags to the kitchen, please, go take a shower, and then go finish reading your books."

"Ah, man," Keaton whined, aggrieved. "Transformers is coming on!"

"Sure, go ahead and watch television. Then when Aretha Skypes you in," he looked at his watch, "three hours and fifteen minutes, you can tell her about Transformers instead of the book report on *Moby Dick* she's expecting you to have completed. That'll work, right?"

Two dejected faces showed the right amount of fear and trepidation about not having finished a book report and trudged away to do as instructed, their grandmother on their heels.

"Quite a handful you've got there," Angelique commented.

"You have no idea, but I'm going to take them to Summer County with me for Thanksgiving for a little southern exposure with the family and give Mrs. Joyner a break. By the time those boys finish mucking out the stables, feeding chickens, gathering eggs, slopping hogs, and currying horses at o'dark thirty in the morning, they'll think reading a book is a gift."

"I'll say. I remember visiting your family's farms in the summer, but I had a really good time."

"That's because Aretha had you out of the house visiting every relative in the known universe.

"Let me get cleaned up before the boys use up all of the hot water. Make yourself comfortable. I'll only be a few minutes."

When he scaled up the steps two at a time, Angelique watched him go. He was a tall, well-built man who seemed incredibly light on his feet. He had a natural spring in his step and he was built like a Greek god, she thought. He had long, strong, well-muscled legs and thighs in running shorts and a T-shirt molding nicely to his well-cut six pack, pecks, and abs. The back of him was as intriguing as the front. She had a hot flash over the thought of him naked, wet, and warm in a shower.

To distract herself she wandered to one of the windows and could see a panoramic view of the East River, the Brooklyn Bridge in one direction and the Manhattan Bridge in the other. She didn't know New York City very well, yet, but she realized Gregory was only a matter of minutes from Wall Street and the Stock Exchange. Just as she thought it, a helicopter rose from the South Street Seaport heading west. New York was such a vibrant city and every neighborhood had something extraordinary to offer.

She took off her ankle boots and sat on the wide, comfortably padded window seat with its array of colorful pillows and an unobstructed view of the river, and the bridges spanning it. She pulled her long legs to her chest, wrapping her arms loosely around them. Bracing her chin on her raised knees, she absorbed the environment's absolute tranquility.

That's how Gregory saw her when he descended the stairs a short time later. She was in profile, but everything about her was luminous. Her long, ink-black hair was in a thick plait starting at the crown of her head and falling to her mid-back with an intricately designed barrette attached to the end. He would have just stood at the bottom of the stairs, leaning against the railing looking at her had the boys not come pushing and shoving each other down the steps.

"Set the table, please," he requested to give them something constructive to do. They had so much energy needing to be harnessed and channeled so he followed them to the round table near the kitchen area by a large window to help set up the food Mrs. Joyner was making. He arranged the electric chafing dishes on a sideboard and plugged them in. While they heated, he removed the cooked food already in Pyrex, square, glass containers from the warming drawers and placed them in the chaffing stands.

Mrs. Joyner removed the last of the home-made biscuits from one of the wall ovens when Gregory walked toward Angelique.

She watched Gregory help set up breakfast with Mrs. Joyner and her grand boys. It was like watching a well-choreographed ballet. Clearly this was a routine repeated over time. Then she watched him walking toward her wearing a pair of faded jeans, a clean white T-shirt, and bare feet. He looked absolutely indescribably delicious, she thought, when he smiled at her and smelled even better.

"Breakfast is ready," he said, taking her hand and helping her up from the window seat. He tucked her hand under his arm and led the way to the table. She felt the warm floor under her sock-covered feet. Keaton stood holding her chair for her to be seated while Dejon seated his grandmother and then said grace.

Angelique imagined the gentlemanly behavior was Gregory's influence on the boys and enjoyed listening to their animated conversation around the breakfast table. Gregory, she noted, had a healthy appetite, still only put small portions on his plate at a time, but went back for seconds. The food was delicious and the light and airy baking-powder biscuits to die for. There were scrambled eggs with Pepper Jack cheese and fresh spinach, thick hot sausages, home fries with onions and garlic, stewed, sliced, cinnamon apples, ice-cold orange juice, and piping-hot, aromatic coffee for the adults and hot peppermint chocolate for the boys. They lingered over their coffees, but when the meal concluded the boys cleared the table and loaded the dishwasher while Mrs. Joyner made her grocery list.

"Anything you need special?" Mrs. Joyner asked.

"Poker game on Wednesday. It's my turn to host. I'm making pot roasts in the crockpots so I need to harvest the celery, onions, carrots and white potatoes. I think I still have cooking sherry. I'll pick up incidentals on the way home, but if you would bake more brown wheat loaves one each of your garlic and oregano bread and onion and thyme or parsley bread on Wednesday, I'd appreciate it. I don't have enough left of what you baked before."

"I can do that. You'll need to get some more kegs of beer for Ms. Margo and Mr. Troy, and bring up more wine for Ms. China and Joyce."

"Thanks for reminding me. I'll make some kind of dip, maybe fresh salsa so I need chips and limes. I'll take care of it, but that should be all. I'm out or working late almost every night next week."

"I'll bring you down some of whatever I fix and stick it in your refrigerator just in case."

"Thanks, Mrs. Joyner."

"Well, now you and my grand boys are out of the bathrooms, let me finish cleaning your bedroom and the baths before I start the laundry. Then I'm off to get my hair, toes, and nails done, and then to the market," she said, rising from the table and heading up the staircase. "I'll drop your suits and shirts at the cleaners and pick up what's ready."

Gregory turned his attention to Angelique. "All right, young lady, let's get started."

With a wonderful meal under her belt, she would have preferred to stretch out on one of the wide window seats again and take a nap. It was still a new sensation knowing she could now eat anything and everything she wanted in moderation without her weight being an issue when she was still modeling or acting in a movie. She was never stick thin, she always had noticeable breasts, a pronounced butt, and a narrow waist, and flat stomach, but now she was wearing a size eight, instead of a size two. She liked feeling more substantial with her height and new weight. Yet, she had a very high metabolism that wouldn't allow her body to put on pounds easily. Still, she continued religiously working out in a gym, keeping to a strict regimen from her days on the runways of the world's top fashion houses. She still needed the stamina to be on her feet all day and into the night at her restaurant.

"Okay, let's see what we're working with here," Gregory said, as he opened the first box. Nothing was in order or in folders so he began by turning on three computer monitors. "We're going to do a number of things at once, but first we're going to scan all of this paper into a program and then assign each one to a file. There are several programs geared to restaurant management and we'll decide which one suits your needs the best."

They began feeding the papers in to an artificial intelligence program that automatically built a multifunctional accounting program. They worked side-by-side for several hours, until the boys clambered down the stairs wearing soccer gear.

Gregory checked his watch. "Okay, let's take a break. It's nearly time for the game." He grabbed his socks and shoes, a team jacket and a ball cap he wore backward on his head.

Angelique had split seconds to put on her ankle boots and her jacket before Gregory took her hand, hurried down the stairs, and out the front door behind the boys. A few blocks down and over, about a ten-minute walk, they came to Battery Park, a twenty-five acre green space, bikeway, and promenade. Gregory pointed out where the park included, on one end, Hope Garden—a memorial to AIDS victims—and on another, the ferry to Ellis Island, the Statue of Liberty, and a number of other memorials and monuments scattered in between. There was also the Shrine of Elizabeth Ann Seton and an area where clipper ships used to dock. He explained the ships were where Negro stevedores would sing their sea songs, called shanties, to earn extra money. Gregory further explained his ancestors were originally seamen who were privateers from Alexandria, a small principality in Egypt. Eventually they came to a wide expanse of land where several soccer fields were installed with earlier games still in progress.

Gregory gathered his young team members and co-captains together to go over their game plan strategy while Angelique found a seat in the packed bleachers among parents, grandparents, and other onlookers. Angelique had once dated a prominent European soccer player, so she was familiar with the game and rules. She cheered along with the others in the bleachers for over an hour. The game ended in a tie, but the kids seemed to have enjoyed themselves. The boys were heading off to a neighborhood pizza parlor with others to celebrate. Gregory again took Angelique's hand and walked among the crowd to the pizzeria. The pleasing scent of oregano and tomato sauce waffling out of the front door was enough to pull them unerringly into the small space. The young soccer players headed for the game machines lining the back wall while the adults found seats and ordered the food. The boys had pizza and pop. Angelique ordered the Chicken Fiorentia all Arancia and Gregory went for the sautéed steak and pasta with a fresh, field-green salad. They both had a glass of wine with their orders accompanied by large glasses of ice-cold water with lemon wedges.

The walk back to the fire station house helped to settle the heavy lunch. While the boys went upstairs to play games or watch television, Gregory and Angelique resumed working on their project. Around five in the afternoon, Mrs. Joyner returned in a taxicab with the groceries, her hair and nails freshly done. Once Gregory's groceries were put away, she collected her boys for their short walk home with her own groceries.

Chapter 4

The day was sunny, breezy and warm, but the night was clear and cool with a strong breeze blowing inland off the river. Fall was coming on fast, Gregory thought as he lit the fireplace and pulled a frozen container of thick tomato and basil soup from his freezer putting it in a pan of boiling water to heat. He built a couple of Italian hoagies while Angelique cobbled together a veggie and pasta salad. He had never invited a woman, other than purely platonic female friends, into his space. He was trying to think of her only as a family member. Though his feelings for her were anything but platonic, he found having Angelique there felt somehow comfortable and right.

Angelique was having similar feelings about Gregory, but then she always had amorous thoughts of him. She fought it, but the simple pleasure of him reaching for her hand somehow made her feel things she had never felt before for any man of her acquaintance. She absolutely loved him and what it said about the insight it gave her about him. His wide open gourmet kitchen with high-end appliances said he liked to cook. She couldn't have designed a better kitchen layout herself and realized JaiHonnah must have converted the fire station into a comfortable, open-concept, ultra-modern home. Jai had designed the restaurant and bar for her and JRock's construction company had done the renovations. Gregory had a lot more space than her three-bedroom, two-bath flat in the apartment building above the restaurant, but he used every inch of his space well. She rented the space because it accommodated her family when they came to visit and it had easy access to her restaurant and bar, but it wasn't as ideal as she would have liked. What Gregory had was a dream home.

"I really like your place," she told him while they sat on large pillows on the heated floor before the fireplace. The round, squat table held the remnants of their meal. "When I arrived this morning, I wasn't sure I had the right location."

He chuckled at that. "Thank you . . . I think," he said, looking around. "As you can no doubt see, it's an old, brick-and-block, concrete fire station built in the late 1800s. From my research, I learned it was decommissioned in the 1940s, boarded up, used as a city storage facility and then more recently scheduled for demolition. A friend lives not far from here and I was visiting her when I spotted this place. I bought it from the city for a dollar and had JaiHonnah and Roderick Baylor's company handles the renovations to convert it into a single-family home. Would you like to see the rest of it?"

"I really would, yes."

"Grab your jacket. We'll start on the roof and work our way down."

Again, Gregory took her hand and led her to the door she noticed before. He opened a panel and pressed a button. She heard gears start to grind and then a chime sounded. When he opened the door she was surprised to see an elevator inside. He pushed a button marked **RT**, the elevator doors closed, and the box began to rise. Soon the doors opened onto a rooftop green grassy deck half covered and glassed in and the other half open to the chilly, night air. It was a surprise to see real grass on the roof deck. They stepped out of the glass-enclosed area to where there was a breath-stealing, panoramic nighttime view of the city skyline in all directions, and across the river. There was a generous amount of attractive outdoor furniture scattered on the grass among potted trees, and other shrubbery, an array of herbs in container gardens, and a high-end outdoor kitchen. When Gregory flipped on one of many switches on a wall panel, an eight-foot-deep, in-deck swimming pool lit from underwater.

"This level and the one below were added on to the original structure and designed to match the façade. The roof is retractable," he said, pointing up to where it was partially covering the grassy deck. "In the summer it can get really hot up here so I close up the roof for shade and privacy, and to activate more of the solar panels, but leave the movable glass walls open to catch the breeze. The trees are growing nicely and provide a bit of shade too. The grass is more comfortable under foot than concrete would be. Since it's getting colder, I'll cover the pool by closing the roof. That way I can still swim in the fall and winter. The floor and pool are both heated and cooled during the spring and summer."

"I imagine it was Jai's idea."

"It was, yes. She and Roderick have the same set up at their office and home in DC."

She took one last look before he turned off the lights and they re-entered the elevator out of the chilled night air.

When they went down a flight, the doors opened onto what was clearly a master bedroom with en suite and sitting areas with sofas, side tables, and lamps. Again the windows were incredibly large with huge expansive wall spaces and more art pieces and tree-sized plants. Still no clutter, but a hint of lemon oil and bees wax clung to the air.

"Heated floors?"

"Yes, and air conditioned too on every level including the garage and roof top so I can use those spaces year round. With the ceiling fans also on every level and in every room, a humidifier and a dehumidifier, it keeps the place comfortable all the time. For the most part this place operates on the rooftop solar panels and geothermal energy on the garage level so I'm pretty much off the city's electric grid. When Hurricane Sandy hit, I didn't lose power the way others around me did. The propane gas, coupled with a rain-barrel system in the garage, makes this place fairly self-sufficient. Again, Jai's and Roderick's thinking outside the box has me covered for most eventualities. The only thing I may need to be concerned about is flooding since I'm so close to the river."

He walked her through and around his closet; one large enough to be considered a boutique. It led to a luxurious master bath with a wide, see-through fireplace that backed into the bedroom wall. Skylights illuminated the space. There was a walk-around shower with healthy, live plants, boulders for benches under several waterfall sprays and, a wide, hot tub that could easily seat eight. A long, back-to-back, his-and-hers vanity and wash station sat in the middle of the room with attached lighted mirrors and medicine cabinets. Benches added convenient seating outside a closed-in commode room. Again, like the rest of his home, there was no clutter. Everything had a place in see-through, finely crafted cabinets and drawers.

She was reluctant to leave the space, but he led her across the hall into a game room with a pool table in the center of the room. A Ping-Pong table, game machines, and Foosball were in the room. Of all things a couple of train sets circumnavigating and crisscrossing the room up high and others around the circumference of a large table complete with miniature buildings and scenery.

On one glassed-in wall of shelves were the trophies he earned throughout his life. His Olympic gold medals, three championship rings, autographed basketballs from teammates, one for each year he played in high school, college, and the pros, trophies, and photographs chronicled each step and stage of his former life.

"*Wow!*" Angelique exclaimed and clapped her hands like a child on Christmas morning. She rushed forward to press her hands and face against the glass to admire his collection and then walked around the lake-size table as Gregory set the trains on the table and above in motion. She stared mesmerized, her eyes alight with pleasure. She didn't know where to look first; at the trains above or the ones on the table. "So, we're under the roof-top deck?"

"Yes," he said, flipping a few switches and automatically opening a curtain to reveal the underwater view of the pool through a thick glass wall.

"Wow!" she said, again, this time breathing the word in absolute awe.

They played with the trains before he led her out of the game room and this time instead of the elevator, they went down the interior teakwood steps to the next level. It contained eight, generously-sized bedrooms, two on each wall, all with attached baths. A large, open-concept, common room in the center had flat screens with various games attached. There were sofas everywhere, yet the space was not cramped or crowded. A kitchenette and bar anchored the room.

"When the family is in town, this level is a madhouse. Chuck and Vivian bring their brood to the city for weekend excursions or to see a show. As you probably know, my niece, Linda, is a prima ballerina and principal dancer who is currently on tour with a dance company in Greece. When she's in town she usually takes up residence in one of these rooms whether I'm here or not."

"I know," she said, and laughed. "She told me when I saw her perform in Paris she's trying to find out who you're dating. Aretha was there, too. We all stayed at your Aunt Mariah's home."

He also laughed. "Don't tell her, but she's SOL because I don't bring my dates here. I never know who in my family may show up. I generally check into a McCoy Hotel if I'm on a date or go to her place. This place I live in and have only family and close personal friends here. I like my privacy and I would lose it if I brought women I've dated here. Not every relationship I've had ended amicably. I never know with any relationship how things will work out." He shrugged. "Plus, some women like having access to room service twenty-four seven, more than they like having access to my body," he joked. "I can feed myself, but I'm not a short-order cook. Some women wouldn't even want to put a meal together with their imagination and own two hands the way we did tonight."

He looked into her beautiful eyes and realized having her in close proximity to eight bedrooms was asking for trouble.

"Speaking of tonight, it's time I got you home. You can see the rest of the place at another time. It's late, but we made a good start today on your accounting records. We'll finish up tomorrow."

She didn't want to go, but also didn't want to test the waters tonight. So when he put his arm around her shoulders and led her down the stairs to pack up her boxes, she made no complaint.

He loaded the boxes into a roomy, late model, black SUV with tinted windows all around. The garage door crawled up and they exited onto the street. It seemed like only a few minutes elapsed before they were pulling under the Porte Cohere in front of her building. Her doorman immediately came out of the lobby to open her car door while Gregory got the boxes from the back.

"Good evening, Ms. Angelique," her doorman acknowledged with a slight bow and a hand to his cap.

"Good evening, Harry."

Gregory carried the boxes and Harry quickly retrieved a trolley.

"I'm going to church in the morning with Mrs. Joyner and the boys and then to their church's Harvest Festival. Still, I'd like to come by tomorrow afternoon around two if it's convenient. I want to install this new software package on your home and office computers. We'll take some time getting you more familiar with how it works and some of its reporting features. I've already done a backup of your records. We can shred these boxes of papers once the system is up and operational. I also need to see what type of equipment you have."

"Two is fine. I should be in the restaurant. Give me a call when you're on your way and I'll make sure Roy is aware you're expected."

"Great, I'll see you then," he said, kissed her forehead, embraced her quickly, and then was gone.

She stood watching his SUV's taillights fade into the thick flow of traffic before she walked through the door Harry held open for her.

She had a wonderful day with Gregory, she wrote in her journal later that night, giving every detail of what she saw, heard, and felt. She had a warm feeling and a smile on her face as she turned out her bedside lamp and snuggled bare-bodied into bed.

Chapter 5

After his early morning run, Gregory settled into his garage to spend a few hours working on a vintage 1955 Pontiac GTO he was bringing back to mint condition as a gift for his parents' wedding anniversary. The car originally belonged to his paternal grandparents and was considered a luxury item when it was manufactured. It and several other vintage cars were in one of his parents' barns along with old farm equipment. His mother was threatening to take a wrecking ball to the barn if his dad didn't clear out some of the "junk" in there. She said it attracted rodents and she dearly hated mice and other vermin anywhere near her home. So piece by piece Gregory planned to restore the old cars and pass them on to his nieces and nephews when they reached the age to drive. He liked working on them. It relaxed him and this morning he needed to relax.

When his oldest brother, Kenneth, made new or refurbished old furniture (also stored in another one of their parents' barns) as he had done in this same garage for nearly every piece in Gregory's home, he found a certain peace of mind practicing the old ways taught and passed down through the ages by the elders from the generations of his family. Benjamin, second in the Alexander line of siblings, helped too, but Benny's talents went to designing and building mechanical things, like aircraft though he learned to carve model airplanes and cars out of wood at their paternal grandfather's knee. Gregory's father, and brothers, Kenneth, and Benny, spent two weeks with him when his home was ready for occupancy. His brothers brought their children with them, but left their wives foot-loose and fancy free while the children learned the old ways from their grandfather, fathers, and uncles. Even at a young age, Benny's oldest daughter, Whitney Ivy, could take an engine apart and put it back together again not leaving out one nut or bolt. Gregory called her his Road Dawg when she came to visit him with her dad and triplet younger sisters. He loved all of his nephews and nieces and having them piling in on top of him and one another in his home was crazy fun for him.

Vivian was reluctant to dump her brood, numbering twenty-four at last count, on him, but since his time was pretty much his own, he would often steal her children on extended minor holidays. He wanted a house full of his own one day. Strangely, every time the thought crossed his mind of late, so did Angelique.

He had imagined her last night in his bed her belly plump with their child. With that image in his head, he didn't sleep much, so he got up extra early for his run. With his music pumping old school funk, he took two turns around the circumference of the World Trade Center between Liberty and the World Financial Center before he hit his favorite bakery for bagels, cream cheese, and lox just after they opened at seven o'clock. He regularly stopped there on his walk to work in the morning.

He noted the time and realized he would soon have to clean up, dress for church, attend the Harvest Festival, and then go directly to Angelique's to install the computer software package and determine what, if any, hardware she needed.

He took a deep breath and let it out slowly. Being with her yesterday gave his growing feelings for her a much deeper, symbolic meaning. He wanted to get to know her better as the young woman she was now before he got in too deep. So far there were no yellow or red warning flags he detected as there were with his dwindling relationship with Alondra. She wasn't clingy, but there was definitely something more she wanted from him beyond a couple of energetic rolls in the hay. Of late, she wanted to come to his offices at CTI to have lunch in the executive dining room rather than to go out to a restaurant. The food was exceptional in their office, no doubt. Most of the partners ate lunch there if they didn't have outside appointments, but her desire to be there uninvited or unannounced sometimes conflicted with his exercise schedule at the sports and health club or other business he had to conduct. His relationship with her was never intended to lead to love or marriage, but in the past week or so it was becoming unsustainable.

"Good afternoon, Mr. Alexander."

"Good afternoon, Mr. Conway. How are you today, sir?"

"Fine, thank you for asking. Ms. Angelique told me to expect you," he said, leading him through the quiet restaurant to a kitchen entrance. When he opened the door, pandemonium reigned. There were white-jacketed people all wearing crisp, white caps and splattered chefs' tunics everywhere shouting it seemed in a multitude of languages and scurrying from one station to another carrying large pots or platters of raw ingredients at the behest of someone in authority.

In the chaos, Gregory spotted Angelique whose whole concentration was centered on the hind quarter of a slab of meat as she hacked it into portions while removing what appeared to be excess fat or gristle. She was speaking rapidly in Spanish to five people who stood around her intently looking on and nodding understanding with their arms folded at waist height with white linen towels over their hands.

She took sections of meat and a heavy, dimpled mallet and began beating the meat into submission. How she could even hear herself think in the loud, chaotic environment was a wonder to Gregory.

Mr. Conway made his way through the madness, eased up behind her, and leaned to whisper in her ear. Her head came up, her eyes seeming a little unfocused, but when she searched the room and her eyes met his, an earth-shattering smile bloomed on her face and went straight to his loins. Her gloved hands were bloody, but their eyes locked and held as she whispered something to Mr. Conway who nodded and rejoined Gregory near the door.

Angelique regained her students' attention, which, for her females, seemed near impossible. Even the males recognized him and were gawking. Gregory made a striking focal point for any female with a pulse. They were a group of Latino at-risk, local male and female youth she was training to work in her restaurant. They had raw talent and showed an aptitude for cooking. She was pleased with their progress so far, but they had miles to go on the academic side to make it into any of the world's top culinary schools. For the time being, she was helping them earn scholarship money and experience toward their goals.

"All right, Pietro, please come and take over here," she called out to one of her chefs de cuisine. He was at her side in moments. "I'll be back shortly. I want this beef carcass to be down to the bone for bouillabaisse and the meat so tender and perfectly seasoned it will melt like ice cream on the tongue."

She stepped back and watched with Pietro for a moment as the students went to work. Then she took off her gloves, washed and oiled her hands, and stripped off her white tunic and cap depositing them in a laundry barrel before she exited the kitchen. Her heart tripped as she met Gregory's eyes over the rim of his coffee cup. He and Mr. Conway sat in the club side of the bar, The Run Way, which was closed on Sundays, but the employees sometimes sat there on their breaks.

He stood when she came to him. His embrace was warm and affectionate. He looked and smelled great. He wore stylish casual clothes as if he stepped off the cover of a fashion magazine. Not many tall men could pull off that look and not be in the business.

"Hi, you," he said, and kissed her forehead.

"Hi, yourself. You look great. How are Mrs. Joyner and her grand boys today?"

"All are well."

"Would you like something to go with the coffee?"

"Thanks, no," he said, patting his flat, firm stomach. "I think I sampled a little of everything at the Harvest Festival. I even bought several bushels of sweet potatoes, corn, and different types of apples."

"Mrs. Joyner also invited me to come. I regret I couldn't make time to go, but, after Mass this morning, I had so much to catch up on because I wasn't here yesterday."

"Well, let's get started first with your home and then your office computer."

She took his hand, feeling comfortable with the incidental, yet somehow intimate gesture and led him out of The Run Way to the service elevator in the back of the building. They went up to the fourth floor and entered a back door to her apartment. Though it was nicely decorated, it was rather small as is typical for Manhattan apartments.

She led him to an alcove, not much larger than a broom closet, where she had a secretariat tucked in behind closed doors. Her computer sat in the middle of the small desk with a pullout shelf below that held her keyboard.

When he sat down before the monitor, he noticed the light of the camera attached to the top changed from yellow to green. Though he didn't mention it to her at the time, it concerned him. Still he booted up her computer and realized it didn't contain the most up-dated software or security package. What concerned him more, when he checked her operating system, was the active and operational spyware he found embedded there. Someone had access not only to everything she did on her computer, but also to her security system in her apartment, restaurant, and club.

"You know, I think I'm going to need to get a few things from an office supply store. Do you have time to take a walk to the store with me?"

Angelique thought the request strange, but shrugged. "Sure. Let me get a jacket," she said, and walked away to what he assumed must have been her bedroom.

Gregory took the time to surreptitiously wander around the living and dining rooms and kitchen noting the number of cameras carefully concealed in each area. He shuddered to think what might be concealed in her bedroom and bath.

When she joined him, they left by the front door instead of the rear. As soon as they were on the street, clear of her building, he put his arm around her shoulders drawing her closely to his side. "What do you know about the security system in your apartment?" he asked, as they walked.

She had slipped her left arm around his waist and was matching his pace. She looked up at him, her brows furrowed. "Not much. I mean it was already installed when I leased the property. I had someone link it to my computer so I could monitor who was in the lobby waiting to see me by looking at my televisions or computer. Why, Gregory? That sounds like a really strange question."

"Someone is spying on you. No, Angel, don't stop. Just keep walking," he cautioned when she jolted and would have stopped.

He explained what he noticed to her building panic.

"Don't worry because this can and will be handled." He pulled his cell phone from his pocket and thumbed through his directory before pressing one button. "Hey, Kenneth, you got a minute?"

"Sure," his brother said. "What's up with you, kid? Didn't I just talk with you via Skype?" he teased. His parents and siblings did a multi-link Skype connection every Sunday morning because they were scattered around the globe. Then something must have alerted him to possible trouble. "Greg, what's wrong? What's happened? Are you secure?"

"I'm fine, yes. I was just at Angelique's place to install a new program on her home computer and link it with her office in her restaurant and club when I tripped over spyware in both her home and office computers. Someone's spying on her."

"What the hell! Give me her IP address," he demanded.

Gregory gave the relevant information to him and in less than a minute Kenneth was in and running a security analysis program on her systems. "Look, Greg, this is bad, really bad. I'm calling Slade Richardson with Richardson Investigations and Security to come in and open an investigation. Don't let Angelique go anywhere near her place. Keep her with you until we can clear this up."

"Done," he said, and then made another call to Adventurer Ground Service. "I need a pickup on this route," he said, as he continued to walk with Angelique closely tucked into his side. Before they reached the next two intersections, his phone started to beep consistently and faster, getting stronger the closer they got to the corner. When they turned onto the cross street, a town car sat double parked waiting with the door already open. A driver was standing by; a side arm holstered under the left side of his uniform coat. The beeping went to a solid tone and ended as Gregory followed Angelique inside the car, then keyed his code into the car's system.

"I don't understand, Gregory. Someone is spying on me?"

"Yes, big time. Your place is full of bugs and so is your computer. As I said, I noticed your Skype camera went from yellow alert to green when I sat in front of the monitor. If it wasn't in use, it shouldn't have done that. When not in use, it should be dark or red. Yellow or green means someone is watching you. Since you didn't personally have your security system installed, I called Kenneth to check it out. He confirmed my suspicions. His company, CompuCorrect, installs security systems on office computers and home systems, among other things. They handle our office computers and our home systems; all of our electronic communications devices. With the sensitive data and clients we handle, we can't afford to have our systems hacked or breached. Because any one of my partners or other employees also work from home or remotely, we have to secure our personal systems as well because we are synced up to the office main frame and cloud."

"I don't understand a lot of what you're talking about, but what can I do to stop this?"

"Kenneth has a contract with Slade Richardson for field investigations and security work. He's putting Slade's company on this today, but he doesn't want you anywhere near your home or business until this is done. Probably by tomorrow Kenneth will have shipped new computers for Slade's people to install and replace what you have. Slade will also eliminate any security problem in your apartment unit and alert the building owner and management about the breach. Since someone is spying on you, they may also be spying on others in the building."

"Is this dangerous? I have employees to consider and a good friend who lives in the building. I don't want anyone to get hurt."

"Not to worry. Kenneth and Slade will get to the bottom of this and turn it over to the FBI to follow up with any necessary arrests."

The car pulled to a stop a block from Greg's home.

"Cell phone?" the driver asked.

"Give your cell phone to him, Angel," Greg instructed.

She dutifully handed it to the driver before they got out of the car and he drove away. At her worried look, Gregory said, "That's just a precaution. I didn't want to tamper with anything and alert whoever is doing this we're on to them. The moment we got into the car, no one could track our movements or destination. It would appear something went wrong with your cell phone signal. Happens all the time. Calls get dropped in certain dead spaces. As far as anyone knows you're still somewhere near your restaurant, club, and flat. Kenneth will have a new cell phone for you with everything he ships to secure your home and business."

"How do you know all of this?"

Though she knew him, he couldn't tell her about his cousin, Donald Dixon, and the role he plays in world security and law enforcement, but he could give her some of the process to help allay her fears.

"People who are often or continuously in the spotlight have a higher risk of being assaulted or abducted or of having their privacy invaded. They have to take certain extra security precautions. Maybe it doesn't happen as often for supermodels, but I can't count the number of times athletes are targeted for any number of reasons. Usually by some jokester or person looking to score something to sell to the tabloids. We, both men and women, learn to be circumspect and use technology to reduce the potential for problems to arise.

"While we were walking down the street I called a security car service on a protection alert line by saying I need a pick up on this *route* indicating I was on the move. If I were to call for a pick up on a non-security issue, I would have called a different number and said, I need a pick up at this *location*, meaning I'm stationary. Both numbers are preprogrammed into my phone. Either way, the car service knows who

I am and locks on to my location, tracking me via my phone's GPS signal and cell towers even if my phone is not on. In most instances, I can be picked up in a matter of minutes in the city just as we were before. I get a beep when I'm nearing the pick-up car and a tone when I get inside. That's when I key in my security code and the dispatcher knows the job is complete. If I didn't find the car, the police would have been alerted and an APB, All Points Bulletin, would have gone out to every sector car in my last known area with a BOLO, or Be On the Look Out for me."

"I heard the beeping, but I just thought someone was calling your phone or you were receiving a text message."

What he didn't mention was he was also tracked via his wrist unit and the gold chain he wore around his neck that read FAMILY. Breaking the chain would transmit an immediate emergency signal. Every family member wore the chain for both unity and security. He took out his phone, directed it toward his home, and pushed a button. Bright exterior and interior lights snapped on. He keyed in another sequence of numbers, placed his thumb on the door strike plate and it opened.

Angelique stepped inside and immediately felt safe, warm, and secure as Gregory reset the security system. They headed up the wide stairs hand-in-hand.

Just as they got to the top step, Gregory's cell phone rang. He recognized the ring tone and was expecting this call to come in the moment he alerted Kenneth to the problem.

"Hey," he answered.

"You secure?"

"Yes, I'm in for the rest of the day and night."

"Yes, I see it on my monitor. You're not alone. I see two heat signatures."

"I have an old friend visiting for a few. You want to say hello?"

"Yes."

"Okay, hold one. Angelique, my cousin, Donald Dixon is on the phone and wants to say hello," he said, passing the phone to her. While they chatted, Gregory went to check his pantry and freezer. He needed to be sure, if he had to leave Angelique alone in his home, she wouldn't need to go out for anything. He didn't know the severity of the problem, but he accepted Kenneth's statement that, whatever it was, it was bad and serious. He also needed to make a few more calls so she would have something to wear for the next few days. He heard her laughing at something his cousin must have said and his blood warmed at the joyous sound. He watched her walk toward him, her face flushed and happy.

"Wait a minute. He's right here. Let me put the phone on speaker."

She did and he heard, *"Playa!"* his cousin's wife, Cecile Jordon Dixon said in her most seductive voice. "I heard you're a playa, Playa. Hello, sweet cakes, I'm the coach."

"Stop it, Cecile, or you're going to get me killed. My cousin loves me like he loves steak and eggs, but he'll kill me dead if he catches me flirting with his wife," he said, laughing.

"The operative words are 'if he catches you,' baby cakes," she teased.

"You're a dead man walking if you even think it," Donald said, in the background.

"He's changing one of his daughter's aromatic diapers, so you're safe for now," said, Cecile.

"I don't have a death wish, brotherman; however if you ever want a boy toy, Cecile and Donald slips up and overdoses on his valium, I'm available." He was only joking, but Cecile was built like a brick shit house. She had real curb appeal, but was a world-class Ph.D. oceanographer with impressive awards and credentials including a Nobel Prize to her credit.

"Hey, just call me a cougar-in-training, young blood," she said, laughing.

"I'm not intimidated. She's very pregnant again, so there is no valium in my future," Donald added.

To Gregory's way of thinking, his cousin was the most calm and collected man in any and all circumstances. He'd make Mr. Spock seem like a jokester.

They laughed, talked more, and hung up about fifteen minutes later.

Two more calls he expected came in rapid succession. First, Bill Chandler said he was in Texas, but would be in New York City in the morning and then his sister-in-law, Benny's wife, Stacy Greene Alexander, a high-ranking, military intelligence officer, called. It had to be about five in the morning in Japan, he reasoned, but she was sharp as a blade with her strategic questions and instructions. He didn't have the vaguest idea of the depth of his family's shadow connections, but he never questioned their integrity or dedication.

He had walked away from Angelique to speak privately with Bill and then Stacy. Now he walked back toward the kitchen area following the enticing aroma of shrimp, onions, garlic and sauce. A pot of water was beginning a rolling boil on the six-burner gas range with center griddle and grill. Angelique was bending forward in his wide-opened, nearly floor-to-ceiling pantry. Her nicely rounded bottom a bit more than his failing control could handle at the moment.

"Do you have Angel Hair pasta?" she asked.

"Uh, yes," he said, and stepped forward to pull a rolling pantry section away, revealing another shelving system behind the first. It was even deeper with more mobile shelves, but he retrieved the pasta from the second section in a clear-glass, wide-mouth jar. "Here you go," he said, handing it to her.

"Wow! You're as well stocked as my restaurant."

"I have to be. I never know who might show up," he said, laughing

She laughed at that. "Yeah, tell me about it. Miguel is always dropping . . ." she trailed off, concern etched on her face.

"Don't worry. I spoke with Bill. He'll take care of security for Miguel, your mother, and stepfather, too. Your brother is in Dallas shooting a movie and Bill is in Fort Worth for contract negotiations for one of his clients. Bill plans to be here tomorrow morning."

"Was he angry with me?"

"No, of course not, just concerned."

"I wouldn't want him upset."

She turned back to the stove to dump a handful of pasta into the boiling water and oil then adjusted the flame.

Gregory pulled a loaf of bread from the bin and sliced it into wide sections. He buttered it, grated garlic and cheese over it, and stuck it in one of the wall ovens to toast the bread and melt the cheese to a bubbling brown.

Angelique was sautéing Brussel sprouts in the butter, onion, and garlic combination before adding the cooked shrimp, shitake mushrooms, and seedless black olives.

The aroma was making his mouth water. The ease and grace with which she moved around his kitchen space was peaking his building desire for her. He turned away, went to his audio system, and loaded several selections starting with Down to the Bone's From Manhattan to Staten to suit his mood. He needed the heady, funky rhythm instead of something soft with strings and harp. Otherwise, he didn't like his chances of being able to keep his hands to himself with her in close proximity. He started to light candles when Angelique asked, "Can we take this up to the rooftop?"

He smiled at her and reached below a cabinet for a four-tiered, rolling cart. *Yes, please.* That was just the ticket to keep his head moving in the right direction. The deck would be chilled, not warm and cozy. Together they placed the food on the cart under domed covers, grabbed a couple of bottles of white wine, and took the elevator up. It was as he expected a bit chilly in the enclosed, glassed-in space, but he soon cured it with the heated floors and the gas fireplace burning cheerfully. They sat at a small round, outdoor furniture glass-topped table just big enough for two and ate by the glow of the candles and the fireplace lighting the space and the up-beat music filtering through the speakers.

It was the most romantic experience Angelique ever had in her young life, she promised herself. Eating under a canopy of stars, city lights, and candles with the man of her dreams across from her, added heat to lust while her heart galloped in her chest.

Chapter 6

Gregory didn't have to wonder for long who keyed in a code and entered his home at this ungodly hour of the morning. The security system automatically announced the name. His immediate family and close personal friends had their own individual access codes to his home and he had similar access to his family members' and friends' homes. He sat on an ottoman near the kitchen, lacing his shoes in preparation for his morning run. Bill Chandler trudged up the steps from the front door hefting what appeared to be a heavy duffle over his left shoulder and another equally large duffle in his right hand. He dropped them both on chairs by the kitchen table, but kept walking shedding his heavy outerwear on his way to the counter.

"Coffee," he pleaded by way of greeting and went straight for the Keurig. He stood in front of the device intently staring at it like a big tomcat watching a mouse hole. His hands were braced on the quartz counter top, his head hung down below his strong shoulders, his startling blue eyes briefly closed, and his healthy, long, brown hair uncharacteristically disheveled. This was a man who still regularly appeared on the cover of every chic, high-fashion magazine in the world. He also owned two magazines, **Risqué,** an outlet for his own line of trendy and stylish clothing, and **Stallion,** a popular gay trade periodical. His extraordinary good looks turned men and women's heads alike.

"I know you said you would be here early, but I didn't expect you until about nine or so."

"As I mentioned last night, I was in Fort Worth negotiating a stalled contract deal. I walked out with my client to give the team's attorneys and owner something to ponder. By hour two they were blowing up my cell phone. It finally dawned on them my client was serious about accepting a more lucrative, multi-year contract with another team. I let them stew for another two hours while I went shopping at Neiman-Marcus for Angelique. Silence is a great motivator and helped them unclench their tight asses. I took my client back to the negotiation table at midnight. He happily signed a very lucrative, multi-year contract at one in the morning. Then he went to celebrate with his lady *de jour* and I got on a jet to come here."

He took the oversized cup of coffee in both hands and brought it to his face. For long, ponderous moments Gregory watched Bill's Adam's apple bobbing up and down, his matinee-idol face buried in the wide, deep cup. No sooner had he finished that cup, he started another brewing.

"While I'm in the air, I had two frantic phone calls from another client, a movie actress who has more body than brains. I had to talk her down from making a complete fool of herself in the middle of a televised awards ceremony in LA. I had just left her hours before I went to Texas after I worked my ass off to get her a spot as one of the presenters. The issue? She saw some other actress' make-up, liked it, and wanted the same artist to do her make-up for a movie that's not scheduled to start filming until late next year. The artist in question refused to even consider it. I know the makeup artist and I can't blame him. While I'm talking with my client's crazy ass, I'm reading a three-hundred page contract I have with another client who wants to force the World Cup soccer team he plays for in Portugal to wear gear worn exclusively by a competing team because he likes that particular shade of purple. I was trying to see whether I left myself an out clause in his contract. Failing that, I've decided I have to hire another junior attorney and pay him or her an outrageous sum of money just to deal with my crazies. Where are all of the sane, level-headed, easy-going clients, like you, I used to have, I want to know?"

When he came up for air after the second cup, he was breathing hard. He stuck another container in the coffee maker to brew for yet a third cup. He regarded Gregory, his brows drawing together. Leaning back against the counter, he crossed his long legs at his ankles and his arms across his muscular chest. "So, what the hell?" he asked Gregory.

"Beats me. I wasn't expecting what I found."

"Angelique wanted to do everything on her own. She's only twenty years old. Damn near still in diapers and she didn't want anyone's help. And, fuck me, I didn't keep an eye on her and what she was doing," he groused, annoyed.

"She didn't go to Joyce or your sister, Margo, either, even though she knows it's what we do."

"Angelique's still so full of gratitude to all of the housemates and, by extension, our families including Chuck's sister and mine, for taking care of her and her family for all of those years. She thinks she shouldn't ask any of us for help now."

"I didn't give her a choice. I didn't intend to, but I snooped and then forced her to let me help her get better organized. Until I got a look at her records, I didn't know it was as bad as it is. In addition to the questionable record keeping, she's put most of her personal resources into her restaurant and bar businesses with no small amount of investment from Miguel. If the business didn't start showing a substantial profit in a year, she would almost be broke."

"Oh, hell. This is my fault for not insisting she let me help her."

"Don't kick yourself, Bill. She has the right idea, but she didn't go the extra nine to plan her strategy and work her plan. It's a common novice business owner's mistake."

"Yeah? Well, your sister is still going to kick my ass for letting Angel get into this mess."

"You heard?"

"Okay, so now what? I don't want to break Angel's spirit, but I'd better have my ducks in a row before Vivian hears about this."

"I think I've got it covered. Angelique is bright and resourceful. She just needs to learn the ropes. I can teach her the ropes."

"You seem to be the only one she'll let help her, but then you've always seemed to hold a mysterious power over her."

"Cut it out, Bill! She's just a kid. I was twenty-nine my last birthday."

Bill's brows drew together. "Have you actually *looked* at Angelique lately?"

Gregory palmed his face and vigorously rubbed his hands against his morning beard. "Yeah, I have, a little too much. She's up on the next level in one of the bedrooms asleep." He pushed to his feet. "I'm out."

Bill shook his head at Gregory's swift departure. "Yeah, brother. Stick a fork in it. You're done. Your goose is cooked." He smirked, turned the next cup of coffee up to his face and drained it.

Gregory slowed his run to a cool-down walk thirty minutes later as he approached the unmistakable Adventurer Ground Transportation town car sitting on the parking pad in front of his home. As he walked in a circle eight, he had a feeling, a bad one, he already knew who else had arrived at his place this early in the morning. He was not anxious to enter his home at the moment, but he had to face the music sometime. It might as well be now.

He heard his sister, Vivian's, deadly quiet voice the minute he opened his front door. That was a tell in and of itself. The angrier she was, the quieter she spoke. She was an even-tempered woman who was slow to anger, but if someone tripped her trigger—duck.

"Why wouldn't you tell me she was trying to do this on her own?!" she challenged marching back and forth while crisscrossing her steps and clearly agitated with her hands planted on her hips. She was somewhere in the midst of her third trimester.

Bill sat on an ottoman, his face buried in his hands, fingers in his hair. "I told you, Viv," his voice a plea for understanding. "I set it up so Angel could have partial control at age eighteen and full control at age twenty. In a minute she'll be twenty-one and legally an adult."

"I don't give a good damn how old she is. She's ours to shelter and protect!"

"Hi, sis," Gregory offered to give the dejected Bill a reprieve.

"Don't you 'hi, sis,' me, Gregory Clayton. I'll get to you in a minute."

"Yes, Madam Justice."

"So, has no one been looking out for her between ages eighteen and twenty?"

"Yes, as her agent, I've signed off on her television appearances, movie roles, modeling assignments, media ad contracts, *etc., etc., ad nauseam*. I'm still acting as her publicist and agent. I made sure her earnings got into her bank accounts and her accounts are audited for tax purposes by our Accounting Department, but I have not monitored how she spends her money. She's a multi-millionaire, but she's always been careful with her accounts. I had no reason to think she would put herself in a bind."

"We're going to make sure she doesn't and her investments don't suffer. And why did I have to hear third hand some lunatic is spying on Angelique?" she asked Gregory turning on what he called Vivian's Jedi-warrior stare.

He threw up both hands in immediate surrender. "Hey, hey, wait one. I went to the top of the food chain as soon as I found the first breach of her privacy. I've talked with Kenneth, Donald, Bill, Stacy and while I was out running this morning, dad and mom called. The only one who hasn't called yet is Aretha Grace ... and," he lamented, "speak her name and she will appear," he said, as his younger sister's face appeared on his ringing iPhone. He turned away from his sister and Bill to answer. It was going to be a hellified day and it wasn't even seven o'clock in the morning yet.

Angelique sat on the top step out of sight, preparing to face her surrogate family. Two of the seven housemates who helped raise her, Bill and Vivian, were already here. From what she could hear of their conversation, which was everything, she was in pretty deep hot water because of her naïveté. Word was spreading she was in trouble. She could expect to hear from the rest of them if not in person, on the phone throughout the day. They were all as precious to her as she apparently was to them. That fact warmed her heart and brought her near tears. Bill, Vivian, Melissa Charles, Alan Lightfoot, David Carter, Gloria Towson, and, though not officially a housemate, Vivian's current husband, Dr.

Charles Montgomery were her surrogate family. When she was a child growing up in the Georgetown house, when the housemates were law students and Chuck a med student, they collectively took care of her and her family's every need, wish or desire.

When she was a young kid, Chuck paid medical, dental, and general health care costs for her, Miguel, and their mother. Bill bought furniture and amenities, like pretty, pricey sheets, towels and blankets for their four-bedroom, three-bath basement apartment in the Georgetown house Vivian provided. Bill also paid for them to attend private schools all the way through high school and two years at Wellesley College and for Miguel at Penn State. He also took her and Miguel on modeling trips, both his and theirs, to exotic locales. In addition to housing, Vivian also arranged for every aspect of their citizenship process to be completed and saw to all of their other legal needs with the police and fire departments concerning their father's murder. Melissa was their fashionista taking them on shopping trips almost weekly with Gloria for clothes and shoes for every occasion. The young law students and Chuck always found plenty things for them to do. They enrolled her and Miguel in a multitude of activities and showed up in force at every event in which she and her brother participated. David was their tutor in English and Alan taught them about all things cultural. They sat with her and her brother nightly while they did their homework and checked it over. School projects were taken on as a household task. The housemates took turns taking and picking them up from the private school they attended and participated as chaperones for all types of activities.

She felt she owed each and every one of them so much and she wanted them to be proud of her for all they invested in her growth and development. What she didn't remember was nothing changed just because she grew up. They were still her surrogate family and she was expected to share with them what she was doing just as they continued to share every aspect of their lives with her and Miguel. They still showed up in force at every milestone of her life.

When Vivian's face appeared at the bottom of the steps silently looking up at her with arms folded over her baby bump, Angelique knew her procrastination period was over. She stood and walked slowly down the steps. They observed each other for a long, humming moment before Vivian opened her arms and whispered, "Enough said?"

"Yes," Angelique answered, and then sighed in Vivian's warm, strong embrace.

"Well, that's it for me. I've got to be on the bench in an hour and a half," Vivian said, and rose from the breakfast table. She was still surprisingly agile for someone in the advanced stages of pregnancy. "You want to fly back with me, Bill?"

"I'm headed for Barcelona for another contract negotiation and then Japan. It's just as easy for me to fly from here to Spain as it is to leave from DC. I'm going to see my sister and take her and Angel out to lunch or dinner. Then I'll crash here or at Margo's place and work for a while until I fly out at about eight tonight."

"Thanks for the clothes and shoes, Bill," Angelique acknowledged.

"You're welcome, sweetheart, but I didn't have a lot of time to be choosy. Neiman-Marcus after closing with a couple of personal shoppers was the best I could do in Fort Worth on short notice. I'll have some pieces sent from Carlos Ortega later today. His new fall line looks great. He'll drool when he hears you'll be wearing some of his creations."

"That will do until I can go back to my place."

"About that," Vivian interjected. "You are to follow everything Kenneth or Gregory tell you to do to the letter. You will not go anywhere near your condo or restaurant until Kenneth or Donald give you an all-clear. Kenneth will handle this breach in your security with Slade Richardson and Gregory will get you on track with your financial package. Listen to him, Angelique. He's my younger brother, but he handles all of my financial affairs. I trust him and so does every one of my law partners because he's extremely good at what he does," she admonished. "We have all invested our portfolios with him. He keeps us on the straight and narrow and on the right side of the IRS."

At Angelique's nod of acquiescence, Vivian hugged her, Gregory, and Bill and was gone.

Bill hefted one duffle while Angelique grabbed the other and took them up the stairs while Gregory cleaned up the remnants of breakfast. Once finished and the dishwasher started, he needlessly took the elevator up to his bedroom to avoid the possibility of seeing Angelique in his T-shirt again. He didn't have anything else to offer her to sleep in the night before, but, when she came down the steps into Vivian's embrace, he wished like hell he had a floor-length robe for her to wear.

She was too sexy by half with her hair undone, the shirt falling off one bare shoulder, the soft cotton fabric defining her body measurements reaching to just above her knees, and bare feet. She had a little-girl-lost look on her face that made men feel as though they should kneel in her presence. Couple the look with her killer Mona Lisa smile on the cover of a magazine, and they were flying off the shelves. He had a copy of every cover she ever appeared on in a file on his computer. There were hundreds of them since she was eleven years old. He told himself he kept them because they were friends, but he was coming to realize it was a part of the deeper, non-platonic feelings he was developing for her. Yet, he had to keep his head on straight and get her out of the fix she was in. Then he could take a step back and evaluate what might be in his future with her.

He got out of the shower, dressed for work, and packed his gym bag with clean clothes, a toiletry bag, and shoes. He felt comfortable leaving Angelique in Bill's care and knew Bill would take her to lunch with him and his sister, but Gregory decided he would come home and get her before Bill left for Spain. Until this mystery was solved, he would not leave her unprotected.

"So someone has been like looking at you naked?" Margo Chandler asked, in her usual uncensored or unrestrained persona across the cloth-covered lunch table from Angelique and Bill.

"Hey, TMI!" Bill said, aggrieved. "Let's have a little decorum here."

"Hell, Bill, it's not like you haven't seen her naked before," Margo smirked at her older brother.

"I don't think about her being naked when she's working."

Angelique laughed at Bill's pained expression. "I wish I could say the same thing about you, too, Bill, but when you take off your clothes to change into another outfit to model, I stop and stare. You've got all those hard, beautiful muscles ... and everything."

"Oh, hell," he moaned. "Remind me to just shoot myself, why don't you?"

"Are you kidding? I've got full-frontal pin-up pictures of you I cut out of **Stallion**. You remember the photo-shoot you did in a horse barn where you were leaning back against a leather saddle wearing black leather cowboy boots, a black Stetson pulled down over your pretty baby blues, your hair loose around your shoulder, and nothing else? There was a stud horse in the background with a full boner. Well, we didn't want to objectify men," she said, with tongue planted firmly in cheek, "but that picture was hanging in every girl's closet at Wellesley. We had measuring tapes and bets going to figure out whose was bigger, yours or the horse. We decided it was a tie. Still, when I came home for holidays, I had to prove I knew you by taking pictures of you while you were asleep," she said, giggling at his pained expression. "I loved the fact you're so buff and usually sleep nude."

"I did exactly the same thing when I was at Brown to prove he was my brother," Margo told Angelique with a self-satisfied nod of agreement. "I made a mint selling candid shoots of him," she admitted.

"That was in your brat phase," Bill countered. "Now you're a sophisticated, young professional who wouldn't think of doing something so perverse to your only brother."

"Wanna bet?" she teased. "Do you know I could pay my golf membership fees with the sale of just one candid shot of you to the right tabloid magazine? Hell, if I could catch you with company in your bed, maybe a *Ménage à trois,* I could buy the whole damn golf course." She and Angelique broke up laughing while Bill buried his face in his hands, a flush warming his smooth, sun-tanned, blemish-free, translucent, porcelain skin.

"Will that be all, Mr. Chandler?" the waiter asked.

"Yes, thank you, Juan. I'll take the check please."

"That won't be necessary. It's already been taken care of, sir, but we do have a few requests for your autograph and Ms. Angelique's if you don't mind?"

His sister and Angelique were talking to each other about other pranks they pulled on him and didn't notice when Bill's brows drew together as he furtively searched the room. He usually didn't let his guard down when he was in public. He was a street-wise kid and a male prostitute from an early age so he knew what to look out for no matter the venue; especially in a high-class restaurant like this one. At one point, he counted his clients among the Nouveau riche.

He agreed to sign the autographs, but took out his cell phone and keyed in a code. Within moments he got two text-message replies from Richardson's security agents who were in the restaurant at different tables and were shadowing him and Angelique.

It was problematic that he didn't know who had paid for their lunch, but he would have a copy made from the restaurant's security cams for analysis while he was headed overseas. He would also have Richardson's people find out about and run background checks as a precaution on everyone in the restaurant from the moment he, Margo and Angelique entered. Facial recognition programs would be run on everyone by his own people in The Nursery. If he didn't have other covert missions to handle in other countries, he would stay and monitor this invasion of Angelique's privacy himself. Still, he was confident the issues involving Angelique were being handled.

After he and Angelique signed several autographs on the restaurant's acknowledgement rack cards, they rose from the table. He noted the agents who also rose, two heading out, a male and female, ahead of him, Margo, and Angelique, and another three falling in unobtrusively behind. The car service driver stood at the open rear car door waiting. The barely noticeable bulge under his left arm alerted Bill he was armed. Bill also carried a weapon in the small of his back and at his ankle. He, too, was ready to meet any eventuality.

Chapter 7

Angelique wasn't sure what to make of the daggers Alondra Martin seemed to be shooting in her direction. After lunch, she and Bill returned to Margo's office to find the Martin woman there. She didn't know Alondra and had spoken with her briefly only one time at her restaurant. She turned away from the woman's malevolent stare to enter a small conference room where she could sit and use the telephone in relative peace, security, and quiet while Bill handled some frantic client's dilemma.

She had never seen so many people whipping around and dashing from place to place yelling about a "buy order" or a "bull market" something or other. They all seemed like they needed a heavy dose of Prozac to her. True, before a big show, like New York City's Fashion Week, things could get pretty hectic back-stage, but it was for a short period of time; a few hours at best. However, these people had all kinds of numbers and figures zipping across reader boards on multiple lines and in changing colors reminiscent of a carnival midway.

She didn't understand anything about the stocks-and-bonds markets except you had to be swift and very skilled to play on that financial level. She knew people who lost nearly all of their money when the market bottomed years ago. She was fairly young at the time and her *momi* was still managing her and Miguel's investment portfolios. Even back then Vivian was helping to guide their paths. She recommended *momi* invest in the more secure bond market, rather than the volatile stock market. Though the return on the investment was lower and slower, it was also more stable, secured, and sheltered. At least she learned a valuable lesson.

Yet, she admired anyone who could think quickly on his or her feet like her brother. He had an interest in finance and actually took classes at Penn State in business and economics. Though he wouldn't be in class this semester while he was shooting a movie in Texas, he was still keeping up on-line with his studies. She tried to do the same thing at Wellesley, but preferred learning the culinary arts at the largest hospitality educational institution, Le Cordon Bleu. It had fifty schools on five continents serving more than twenty thousand students annually. She preferred that milieu rather than completing her academic career at Wellesley College. She wanted a career as a restaurateur and chef and now was exactly where she wanted to be.

It was a bit disconcerting to learn from Pietro Alahandro, her chef de cuisine, she was not missed on Sunday night and everything was running smoothly so far. According to their booking assistant, reservations indicated they would have a full house for all three of tonight's seatings. Pietro decided to feature authentic Louisiana cuisine. *Of course he would*, she thought without heat. It was his opportunity to shine. After all he was Portuguese and Creole from New Orleans, Louisiana. The menu would include Étouffée, oyster soup, and tomato and okra gumbo. A tossed green salad and then the pièces de résistance: a platter would offer a choice of Chicken Esplanade, Blackened Redfish with crabmeat, parsley rice and shrimp Scarlett with Andouille. Tournedos Rhys with Béarnaise and Marchad de Vin sauces and bouquetière vegetables to be shared. Also being served is his personal favorite and specialty for dessert, Crepes Fitzgerald with fresh strawberry and raspberry sauce toppings. Each course would be accompanied by Pouilly Fuisse and Louis Jadot, her current signature house wines.

Although the menu and sample platters were a departure from her routine, she couldn't argue with his choices. They were excellent. He even laid out a plan for the rest of the week ... in case she wanted to take a little more time off to rest and relax. That was the cover story she gave her staff; she was taking a little vacation. In fact, he had pretty much filled in a fourteen- day menu she admitted, even to him, was intriguing. She knew Kenneth and Gregory didn't want her to go anywhere near her restaurant and bar or flat for the next few days, but she would have to find a way to have a sample of the food delivered to wherever she was to stay.

When she ended the call with Pietro, satisfied with what was going on in her absence, she continued to sit and absently watch the controlled chaos unfolding on the other side of the soundproof glass wall. She assumed the people sitting in cubicles were junior traders or stock brokers. She could see most of them over the half walls surrounding each of them, most talking on telephone headsets, some using two phones on their heads at once. Their eyes roamed the stacked tickertape which constantly rang high on the wall around the circumference of the room on reader boards and appeared to represent markets in different countries and the United States.

Ever so often people would get excited and jump up waving bits of paper until a roaming person would come and record something into a hand-held device. Then they and others would stand and watch the boards for some type of change. High-fives would abound between junior traders. There were flat-screen monitors strategically placed around the room showing different telecasts seeming to change periodically.

"I'm sorry to hear about what's going on with you, Angelique," Joyce Montgomery said, as she came into the conference room and sat down at the table.

"Thanks, Joyce. It is a bit unnerving, but it's being handled, I'm told. So, let's talk about only pleasant things. How are you and Peter coming with setting the date for your wedding? I'm anxious to help you pick out your gown and the bridesmaids' dresses."

"Next topic," she said, and then held up a finger. "Two hundred shares of CM Products at sixty-two per share," she said, into her face mic, then turned back to Angelique though her eyes were constantly in motion scanning the reader boards. "I think it's time I give Peter his freedom. He's decided to stay in Australia for two years so he can crew a sail boat for a regatta."

"Oh, no, Joyce," Angelique said, sympathetically. "I'm so sorry to hear it. I remember you telling me last year he was designing new sails and rigging for some company out of France, but you thought he would be back in country this year."

"That was his plan," she said, momentarily looking at the engagement ring on her finger. "I thought by now we'd be married and expecting our first child."

"Do you think maybe you can work it out? I mean, I remember when Gregory introduced you to Peter your first semester at American University. You two were so much in love."

"I was barely seventeen years old. Do you realize how long ago it was? Ten years. Peter put this engagement ring on my finger a year later. We were both still in undergrad. Don't get me wrong, Angelique, I love him more today than ever, but I can't be as patient as you've been waiting for Gregory to take notice."

Angelique smiled. "He told Bill he has been thinking about me a little too much lately. He's been so affectionate the past few days, but I'm reluctant to hope he has stopped thinking of me as his little sister," she said, candidly.

"You should see yourself. You still have a vivaciousness about you when you talk about him. Greg's perceptive. I'm surprised he hasn't seen how you feel about him."

"I don't think he wants to see it or maybe I'm just not his type."

"I don't believe it for one moment. It's true he's very selective about whom he dates, but I don't think he has a 'type' or doesn't find you attractive. He also doesn't date more than one woman at a time. He looks like a walking wet dream and a helluva ball player, but he's not a *playa*. Right now he's dating Alondra Martin," she said, derisively, "so his reaction or lack of reaction to you may simply be a matter of timing."

"You don't like her?"

"No, I don't and I especially don't like her for Greg."

"Do you think he's serious about her?"

"He has been dating her for months, but he hasn't taken her home to meet his family, so I'd say the answer to that question is a resounding no."

"So what are we going to do here?" Angelique asked, as they walked the long halls through a tunnel leading to the basketball court at the ground-floor level of The Meadowlands sports arena.

"I agreed to do color commentary for a certain number of games during the season. Today is one of the kick-off games for the new season."

"What is that? Color commentary?"

"Simply talking about the game, players, and other teams in the conference, giving an evaluation of their performance as compared to others."

"You get paid for doing it? For just talking?"

He chuckled. "Yeah, go figure."

"Are these the same people you played with before you retired?"

"No, these are NCAA college players; not the NBA," he said, as they came to another check-point where security compared their badges to an electronic list and then passed them on to the sidelines courtside.

Media technicians were setting up camera angles, team student assistants were arranging chairs, placing water bottles for easy access, and the arena crew was giving the hardwood floor another cleaning with wide, soft, white mops. Angelique noted there was a beehive-like atmosphere in the huge arena.

Immediately a tall, broad-shouldered man approached leading with his right hand, a Colgate smile in place. "Greg Alexander, aka Alexander the Great in the basketball Hall of Fame, I'm Brent Howard. I've admired you as a player and person for years. It's a distinct honor and pleasure to meet you. I understand we're going to be paired together this season..."

Gregory shook his hand and noticed it had gone limp. Brent was staring at Angelique slack-jawed. This was a classic reaction when men first saw Angelique up close. Gregory shook his head. What could he say? If a man didn't go off the rails after seeing Angelique, there were some brain cells missing. "Brent Howard, may I introduce my friend, Angelique Menendez-Gaza?"

"Uh," he uttered still star-struck.

Others in the busy arena were now turning in their direction, staring, and then making a beeline with cellphone cameras in hand pleading for

Angelique to pose with them for selfies. *This is going to be a long night,* Gregory knew.

"Why does that man keep turning around and looking back here?" Joyce Montgomery wanted to know from no one in particular.

Margo Chandler launched another piece of popcorn into her mouth. "He's looking at Angel," she said, and gave him a coy smile and a little finger wave, "but he's kinda hot."

"Isn't he supposed to be working or something?"

"Yeah, he is, but Greg is having to carry the show. He's doing both the play-by-play and the color."

"He's really good, isn't he? Gregory, I mean," Angelique said. She was sitting on the first row of seats between Margo and Joyce and directly behind and across the aisle from Gregory and Brent Howard who were courtside.

"You want something from the snack bar?" Dejon asked, over Angelique's left shoulder.

"No, thank you. Do you need money?"

"Gregory already gave us a budget and money for snacks."

"Okay, but do you need me to go with you?"

"Like what, to hold our hands? Get real." The boys smirked, laughed, and got out of their seats to make their way to the long flight of stairs.

She guessed they didn't need her to act as a chaperone.

"Wow, those boys are really doing better. A year ago you wouldn't get a word out of them sideways with a crowbar," commented Joyce.

"Gregory's and Aretha's influence. They were actually on time when we went to pick them up tonight to come to the game," agreed Margo.

"Mrs. Joyner mentioned Gregory told them, if their homework wasn't done, not to bother to come tonight."

Margo chuckled. "Mrs. Joyner said they came straight home from school and hit the books."

"They have to fax it to Greg and he checks it before they go to school the next morning."

"He's very good with children," said Angelique. "I've seen him with his nephews and nieces before."

"He's going to be a great father someday."

Yes, he is, thought Angelique, and she wanted to be the one having babies with him as his wife. Just then, Gregory turned around and looked in her direction, but, she noted he was just trying to get Brent Howard to pay attention to what they were doing.

"Did you enjoy the game?" asked Gregory later that night as they walked out of the arena toward the waiting car.

"I did, yes, once Margo and Joyce explained what was going on. I haven't attended many basketball games before except yours when I was younger and I've never been that close to the action."

"What did you think, Dejon?"

"It was al 'ite, I guess."

"Keaton?"

"How do you get to do what you do? I mean, how do you get to talk on television like you did?"

"There are a number of ways. For example, taking communications-related courses in college and maybe grad school. Then maybe working for a radio or television company, like the nightly sports news or ESPN. I was asked to do the color commentary because I've had years of experience playing the game."

"I know. We used to watch you all the time on television. You were awesome, but you didn't go to school for it, right?"

"That's right. I went to college and grad school to learn about business, finance, and economics."

"Now you know a lot about stuff and sports, too?"

"Yes, I do, but I've always wanted to work in the financial markets."

"I want to be on television," said Keaton.

"Doing what?"

He shrugged his shoulders. "I'on't know. Talk about stuff the way you do."

"It's just as important working behind the camera as it is to be a television personality. Work hard and study all aspects of the communications industry and you can make a better decision about what you want to do as a career."

"Do you, like know other people who work on television?"

"I do, yes. The industry is called broadcasting or cablecasting or videocasting. Now there are other venues like podcasting. If you're seriously interested, I'll introduce you to some of the people I know. They will give you advice and share how they started their careers."

"Cool," Keaton said, as they piled into the back seat of the hired town car.

Chapter 8

"That was a great game you called last night," said Troy Jackson, one of Gregory's CTI partners. They were also related by marriage through Greg's sister, Vivian, and Troy's deceased brother, Derrick. "You done good, Brah."

They were sitting on a bleacher watching a game in progress while they laced their shoes in preparation for their game to follow.

"Thanks. Yeah, I enjoyed it more than I thought I would. That kid out of the Midwest was on fire."

"I see good things happening for State this season."

"I forgot you graduated from Florida State University."

"Played all four years there, too, but I mostly rode the pine," he said, laughing. "My brother, Derrick, had all the athletic and academic talent in the Jackson family." He sobered somewhat in memory of his deceased, sports icon, older brother, Derrick, also known as 'Dunk and Jam' or 'DJ' Jackson. "Here I am following in his footsteps again. He really knew his way around an investment portfolio."

"I know what you mean. I had big shoes to fill, too. Your brother and my sister weren't married long, but for the years I did know him, I thought he was a phenomenal ball player and genuinely great guy. Otherwise I wouldn't have let him marry my sister," he said, and laughed. "Seriously, though, his basketball skills are unmatched even today. He set records no one will be able to better."

"You sure as hell tried," Troy said and laughed, pounding Gregory on his arm.

"Hey, I was just trying to uphold the family tradition," he joked.

"You sure were, but who was the babe you were with last night?"

Gregory looked at him quizzically trying to determine why he didn't know. Then it dawned on him. "That's right; you weren't in the office yesterday. Angelique Teresa Menendez-Gaza went to the game with me last night."

"*That's Angel?*" he asked, disbelieving. "*Dude!* Please pick a lane and stay in it," he joked. "You always score the best babes."

"It's not like that. We're just friends."

"*Seriously?* The camera kept panning in her direction. She's extremely photogenic, but I thought it was because the movie actor guy was sitting behind her in the audience. You were doing the show, but you never mentioned anyone in the audience."

"I couldn't take my eyes off the real estate. I was getting a lot of chatter from the television network director in my ear because Brent's head wasn't in the game."

"Yeah, I noticed. He kept turning around looking in the bleachers behind you." He laughed. "Now I know why."

Just then Gregory's cell phone chimed. When he looked at the text message, he zipped his duffel bag closed. "I'll have to catch up with you another day," he told Troy. "Tell the others something came up and I had to jet."

"Will do," Troy said, as Gregory made a hasty retreat to the locker room to change into his street clothes.

Sometime later, he was at his home climbing the steps two at a time. His brother, Kenneth, came forward and they embraced tightly. Kenneth was the most senior of the first cousins in their generation. The Dixon twins, Donald and James, were born mere months later. To date their family numbers were legion.

"Sorry to pull you away, but I wanted you to meet Slade Richardson and hear his report first-hand."

"Not a problem. I was at the gym getting ready for some exercise. I had a few things on my afternoon scheduled, but nothing I couldn't move to another day. Where is Angelique?"

"She's upstairs on the phone with her mother and stepfather. Fenster was thinking of canceling the rest of his European tour to bring Anna home, but Angelique didn't want him to do it. He's got another six performances in three countries before he has a break just before Thanksgiving. They're in Sweden now. I think Vivian talked them out of coming back early."

"She's here?"

"She and Chuck, too. Chuck wanted Vivian to rest for a while at least until you got here. They're upstairs. Aretha came in sometime after you left for work this morning."

"She said she was coming. She just didn't know when. So where is Richardson?"

"He's flying in from his west coast headquarters in Portland, Oregon."

Gregory looked at his watch. "Spaghetti marinara, a field-greens salad, and garlic toast? There is pie left, too."

"That'll work. I'll raid your hydroponics garden and do the salad and garlic bread," Kenneth said, as they both removed their jackets and rolled up their sleeves. They washed their hands and got to work.

"How are JeNelle and the boys?"

"They're all fine. We're expecting."

Gregory laughed. "You and Donald going for some type of record? Cecile is pregnant again, too."

"We're in good company. You must not have read Aretha's blog lately. James and Janice are also expecting."

"You're right, I haven't. These things involving Angelique have been all-consuming. Is this going to be another one of those occasions when a number of Alexander babies are born on the same day?"

"Not this time I don't think. It was uncanny the way it happened before."

"Yeah, but I can't forget it was the same day Derrick died holding little DJ."

"April Fool's Day of all days. So much joy and sadness at the same time. When you sent the text to me today, I was at my club preparing for a lunch-time game with Troy Jackson. We were talking about DJ."

"Is he okay?"

"Yeah, Troy is fine. I think Derrick's death just hits us all in the gut ever so often. Troy was at Florida State and I was still at UVA at the time in the midst of March Madness when Chuck called to ask me to come to DC to be with Vivian."

They continued talking while making lunch. Shortly, nearly seven-foot tall Dr. Charles 'Chucky P' Montgomery, former stand-out basketball player turned Emergency Room medical doctor, ambled down the wide stairs rubbing his hands together.

Gregory and Chuck clutched in a one-arm embrace. "How is Vivian?" Gregory asked.

"At least she's napping. She hasn't been sleeping very well. I had to give her a massage to relax her. Your sister, who is the center of my existence, thinks she's the first born to Superwoman."

Both Kenneth and Gregory laughed.

"She is. Her name is Sylvia Benson Alexander."

Chuck also laughed. "Yeah, you're right. Your mother is Superwoman personified. Something smells great. Don't tell me mom is here, too."

"Not in person. Spaghetti marinara with meat sauce. Her recipe. It's the best I can do on short notice, but if you want something different I can order out."

"Spaghetti sounds great to me. I need the carbs to keep up with my wife. Got any cold beer?"

"Beverage cooler, bottom rows. There should be some left. I have more in the cooler downstairs. Grab one for me while you're at it, please."

"You want one, KJ?"

"No, thank you. I'll have red wine," answered Kenneth.

For a big, tall man, Chuck moved easily, clearly comfortable in his own skin. Of course anyone would feel comfortable in Gregory's spacious home. It was designed with the statuesque person in mind.

Chuck could have passed for clean-shaven Johnny Depp except for his thick, medium brown long and tied-down hair at the nape of his neck not to mention his impressive height. The diamond stud in his left earlobe gave him a rakish persona. He had a love of cowboy fashion displayed by the many Stetson hats he owned and the genuine cowboy boots he habitually wore even in the hospital. His plaid shirt hung open over a white T-shirt and jeans with a wide intricately designed rodeo buckle at his toned six-pack and narrow waist.

He was an expert Emergency Room physician who, with a few other doctors, owned and operated Physician's Hospital in rural Prince George's County, Maryland; an area adjacent to Washington, DC. He also still had privileges at Georgetown Medical Center where he did his residency and was, at one time, Chief of Emergency Medicine. That was also where he and his life-long best friend, Dr. Derrick Jackson, both met and fell in love with the same young law student, Vivian Lynn Alexander.

Chuck actually met Vivian first in Chicago's O'Hare Airport during a record-breaking blizzard and was falling for her hard from the very beginning. However, at the time she was engaged to another man. When that relationship ended on a sour note, Chuck wanted to allow Vivian a chance to get beyond her hurt and disappointment before expressing his interest in her. He was preparing to do just that when he asked his best friend, Derrick, to join them and the other housemates one night at a country-style dance club, The Red, Hot and Blue. It was a running joke Derrick was a dead-on clone for actor Denzel Washington in his youth, but Derrick took one look at Vivian, who resembled actress Jada Pinkett-Smith, and, as they say, *ball game*. Two years after they met, Derrick proposed marriage and Vivian, who was unaware of Chuck's feelings for her, accepted.

Derrick died less than a year after he and Vivian married. She was twenty-five years old at the time. He was only thirty-seven, but he had a heart ailment, hypertrophic cardiomyopathy, which ended his stellar professional basketball career when he was at the top of his game. Since puberty, Derrick and Chuck were closer than brothers. Their families were also close. Chuck's older brother, Bob, married Derrick's older sister Sheila and they had four children at last count. When Derrick first learned of his condition, he told only Chuck and swore him to secrecy. Ironically, it was Chuck who found Derrick dead in the hospital nursery with little Derrick Junior in his arms. For over an hour Chuck worked on Derrick, but couldn't revive him.

When Chuck told Vivian her husband, and his brother-in-law, and best friend was dead, Vivian was inconsolable. When she asked how this could happen to a man as young and physically fit as Derrick, Chuck revealed the truth about Derrick's heart condition. Vivian was angry with Derrick and Chuck for keeping the truth from her and, as a result, even though Chuck was the executor of Derrick's massive estate and Derrick Junior's godfather, Vivian refused contact with him for five years.

Everyone in her family, his, Derrick's, and friends knew Chuck was still very deeply in love with Vivian and conspired behind her back to give Chuck chances to visit with his godson, little DJ, and the rest of the children Derrick and Vivian adopted or planned to adopt before his death. Vivian, with her extraordinary wealth, continued adopting abandoned, health-challenged children after Derrick's death. Derrick, a pediatric surgeon, owned the lion's share of his twelve-person medical practice which Vivian inherited, so she had an unfettered access to the best medical care for her heath-challenged children.

Finally, on the occasion of Derrick Junior's fifth birthday, he let it slip his 'Uncle Chuck' bought a pony for him for his birthday. That's when the conspiracy came to light. Vivian had no choice but to forgive Chuck for keeping Derrick's secret and revealed part of her hurt, anguish, and disappointment were caused by being in love with him. She felt she was betraying Derrick's memory and thought Chuck never seemed romantically interested in her. Nothing could have been further from the truth. When all of the bitterness dissipated, Chuck and Vivian admitted their love for each other and were married without delay. Trust of each other had been fundamental to their successful interracial marriage. They were an über wealthy couple who continued to adopt abandoned, health-challenged children and live on a working farm. They hired people to work their farm who were down and out and living in the same family homeless shelter where they first found Anna Menendez-Gaza and her children, Angelique and Miguel.

The three men were seated at the kitchen table when Aretha, the youngest of Bernard and Sylvia Alexander's five children, descended the stairs.

"How did it go?" Kenneth asked his youngest sister, Aretha Grace.

"As well as we could hope. Anna and Fenster will stay on tour and come to Goodwill for Thanksgiving. We promised to keep them in the loop about what the investigators find. No one mentioned anything about Angelique and the financial stress she's under. The knowledge would have been the cherry on the icing for them. They would have come immediately. They're on a three-way with Miguel now so I left them to it. When does Richardson arrive?"

"Anytime now. He sent a text stating he's landed. He'll helicopter to the South Street Seaport. It's not far from here."

"Good because whatever you're cooking smells like something I want right now."

Just as the front door bell chimed, Angelique was coming down the steps. Her eyes were red rimmed, but connected with Gregory's when he rose to answer his front door.

When he returned, he was accompanied by a tall, strikingly-handsome man with a beautiful, smooth, olive-brown complexion and thick, black, glossy hair. He looked like the actor Sendhil Ramamurthy from the primetime shows Heroes and Covert Affairs. He could easily pass for someone of Arab or East Indian extraction, but not quite. Slade Richardson stood at least a svelte six-five, but clearly had all muscle cleverly concealed in his custom-tailored, Italian suit. This man did not buy his clothes off the rack. For someone who just arrived in New York after a long flight from Portland, Oregon, there wasn't a wrinkle on him anywhere. He had clear, sharp eyes quickly sweeping his environment, unperceptively so.

"Slade?" Vivian asked, as she waddled down the steps and walked toward his back.

He turned at the sound of her voice. "Vivian," he said, gathering her in for a warm embrace. "It's great to see you again."

"You too. Where is Ash?"

"The Netherlands adjudicating a case involving mineral rights."

"I didn't know you knew Slade," Kenneth interjected to his sister while shaking Slade's hand.

"I met Slade and Thomas Ashton Marshall, Ashton, years ago when I was still a practicing attorney and had a case before the World Court in The Hague, Netherlands. Ashton and I were co-counsel. Our client was France. Slade and Ashton grew up together in Portland. He's the investigative arm of Ashton's law firm Marshall and Marshall, PA. Ashton's grandmother, Esmeralda Marshall, is a former investigative reporter and television commentator. She and I are members of the board of One Thousand Women." What she didn't mention, but Gregory already knew, was Richardson Security provided protection for Vivian's Adventurer air and ground transportation services. Gregory handled her financial affairs, but before now hadn't made the connection.

"Slade, let me introduce you to my husband, Charles Montgomery, my brother, Gregory Alexander, and sister, Aretha. This is Angelique Teresa Menendez-Gaza."

He shook hands with each in turn, but when the front door opened and closed again everyone turned to stare.

"At ease," Donald Dixon ordered as he came up the steps.

"Hey, cousin," Gregory said, perplexed at his unexpected arrival. "I was only joking about being available should Cecile want a boy toy."

"My wife wasn't kidding," he said, and laughed. "She's unhappy with the hours I have to spend out on the road so she's threatened to bring in a substitute husband. We'll have to make this quick or she'll make good on her threat. Come here little bit," he said, grabbing Aretha and then Vivian for a hug. "KJ, Greg, Chuck" he acknowledged with strong clasped right hands, shoulder bumps, and one-arm grips, before taking Angelique into his arms. "How are you holding up, Angel?" He palmed her face and kissed her forehead.

Her eyes watered even though she smiled. "Gregory has been taking very good care of me."

"That's to be expected. You're precious to him and to all of us," he said, and then turned his enigmatic stare on the only person in the room who was not family by birth or marriage.

"Sir," Slade said, with deep deference, seeming to almost snap to attention or genuflect. That alone seemed to surprise everyone in the room, except maybe Aretha.

"Slade," Donald acknowledged just short of calling him by his Nursery Code Name: Cobra Khan.

Then turning to the group at large, he said, "First, let's get whatever is cooking with garlic and not enough oregano on the table. I'll bet there aren't enough black olives and hot peppers in the salad either. Get the garlic and onion breads out of the oven before they burn. Then we can talk with full stomachs."

"Hey! Next time get here before we start cooking and you can do the honors."

"Next time don't start cooking until I get here."

"Like someone ever knows when or where you're going to show up," Vivian groused without heat. "A body could starve and I'm eating for two."

Donald just grinned at her and patted her tummy.

All eight settled comfortably around the table speaking amicably and laughing until the meal concluded and dishes were cleared. They lingered over their beer, wine or coffee while Vivian had water.

"Tell us what you've found," Kenneth directed Slade getting down to the business at hand.

"We found multiple video and audio listening devices throughout Angelique's condo and office in the restaurant, even in the bathrooms and kitchen. The UNSUB placed relay apparatus in the air vents so the signals go multidirectional on Ethernet Wi-Fi connections. We traced eighteen signals, but they led only to other concealed relay locations spread out all over the area. We're following up with the signals leading oconus; outside of the continental United States. We have left the devices in situ while we continue to trace the signals to their origins just as Gregory did. That was exactly the right thing to do, Gregory, by getting you and Angelique out of your apartment without fanfare."

"So you still haven't found out who is doing this?"

"We have an idea it's Stanton Durant, III."

"Stan? Why would he do something this despicable?" asked Angelique.

"It is apparently common knowledge in certain circles he is obsessed with you. He's British royalty so we have to be circumspect about how he is handled, but he has been under surveillance since this alert started. There are some inconsistencies between what we've found and his activities. After you gave him the slip more than six months ago in Paris, he's been employing social media to track your activities. Most recently, you were in the stands at a Little League soccer match watching Gregory's team while they played. After the game you went to a pizzeria. I won't bore you with details of what you and Gregory had to eat and drink, but suffice-it-to-say since you're a Le Cordon Bleu-trained chef, the world is commenting on your dietary choices. However, on the local front, the booth where you sat is now roped off and considered a place of honor."

"Ah, Christ," Gregory groaned. "I don't want my young team members harassed."

"We've alerted the school and the parents."

"Good."

"Then, of course, Angelique, you were in a restaurant with Margo Chandler who works with Gregory, and your agent William Chandler, Esq. So your picture was plastered on certain websites tracking celebrities.

"You have a very dedicated and loyal staff, Gregory. There was not one picture of Angelique in your offices after she, William, and Margo Chandler returned from lunch. However, last night you were at the game in The Meadowlands, Angelique again with Gregory and his friends and partners, Margo Chandler and Joyce Montgomery. There are pictures galore. Rumors have started the two boys Gregory mentors, Dejon and Keaton Joyner, are actually your 'love children'."

"That's crazy!" Angelique exclaimed, annoyed. "Dejon is thirteen! I'm almost twenty one!"

"Details," said Aretha Alexander blithely. "All any enterprising soul will have to do is dig back in my blog history to come up with pictures of all of us together when you first came to America from Peru. The tabloids will have a field day. I can see the headlines now: *Sports Icon and his Child Bride.*"

"They already are," Kenneth said, as he finished searching headlines on his laptop. "Apparently, you and Gregory have been secretly married for years and timed your retirements to coincide so you can now live with your children in the open." He turned his laptop so everyone else could see the tabloids.

"See? There you go and how come I didn't know you were still dating the Olympic Gold Medalist Alondra Miller before you dumped her for Angel?" Aretha asked her brother as she, too, checked certain websites on her iPad. "I'm your sister. I'm supposed to be the first to know these things."

"Oh hell, excuse me a moment. I need to give Alondra a heads up," he said, before rising from the table.

"What can be done to stop this craziness?" asked Angelique.

"As you probably know, once rumors start circulating, regardless of how fictitious or ludicrous, they can morph into reality for some people. For now, the tabloids and social media should simply be ignored or used to your advantage. In my opinion, it's more important we lock down who exactly has breached your privacy and eliminate the threat to your security. My agents are continuing to follow up with tracking every location the signals goes. Whoever is doing this has deep pockets though and could keep us running into blind alleys, metaphorically speaking, for quite a while. This is no fly-by-night or amateur operation."

"I presume you've ruled out the tabloids?" Vivian asked.

"I have, yes. If they were involved, intimate pictures of Angelique would have already been plastered on their front covers. This is personal for whoever is behind this. No other tenants in the building are being watched.

"We've interviewed everyone who has access to your apartment and business. There have been no notable incidents with the exception of Mr. Durant's efforts to get in to see you. He hasn't used force, but he has unsuccessfully tried bribery. He is in this country legally and hasn't broken any laws we're aware of. His behavior does not qualify as stalking. However, we are working through certain people in the British Embassy to encourage him to leave you alone and to leave the country." What he did not share was they were using other female operatives of his acquaintance to attempt to distract him to the point he would cease and desist his attention to Angelique. So far, Plan A was not working, so they were considering Plan B.

Gregory rejoined the group, his thoughts troubled. Alondra demanded he step up his involvement with her by moving in together and sever all contact with Angelique as a means to stop the rumors. He did not appreciate her position or tone and made a spot decision he would stop seeing her instead of Angelique. In his view, his commitment to Angelique was far greater than to a purely sexual relationship with Alondra. She was, apparently, not expecting this particular turn of events and attempted to backtrack on her adamant position. However, she had overplayed her hand and he determined, in light of the situation, and, for all concerned, his decision was irrevocable.

He couldn't say he was particularly sorry to end the intimacy between them. Nevertheless, he tried in vain to offer a continuation of their platonic friendship.

The next sound he heard was a dial tone.

"Is everything okay?" Angelique quietly asked. He had held her hand under the table during Slade's recitation of the facts. She claimed his hand again now and gave it a light squeeze.

"Everything is fine, yes," he said, with a smile to help eliminate the worry on her face.

"I don't want to cause you trouble."

"Not to worry. We will get through this together."

Her battered heart nearly burst out of her chest with his comforting assurance she wasn't alone. Then she had only to look around the table to see she was not ever to feel alone. They—her surrogate family—showed up again when she was in need of moral support.

As she suspected, each of the former housemates, Alan and Melissa Charles Lightfoot, David and Gloria Towson Carter, Chuck and Vivian Alexander Montgomery, and, of course, Bill Chandler, called or arrived in person to offer whatever she needed. Their homes were always open to her to get out of the city for a while; no questions asked. They forced her to agree she would come to Washington, DC, if the situation didn't improve.

Her mother was so racked with fear because her first husband, Angelique's and Miguel's father, was murdered by agents of an evil man, Michael San Angelo, to keep him from revealing a long-held secret. The fact Anna's first husband, a simple farmer and sheep herder, was trying to do the right thing and get information to the proper authorities in Washington, was the reason for his murder. Anna's fear of something similar happening to her children caused both Angelique and Miguel to promise to come to her if anything else happened.

"So we considered letting the tabloids work in your favor for a change."

"How so?"

"Since they and the social media think you and Gregory are the current hot couple, let them. Heretofore, you two haven't been seriously or romantically aligned with anyone else, so let the press and news media believe it's true you're a couple."

"Your theory is the UNSUB will lose interest if he or she believes they are an item?" asked Chuck.

"Yes. If it's Durant, he won't want to be made to look the fool to his peers and will simply back away."

"Or, whether it's him or not, the person will step up the pursuit."

"There is that possibility. The bottom line is we have to bring this state of limbo to a quick head."

"Using me and Angel as bait," Gregory said, drolly.

"There are other options, of course, but I doubt Ms. Menendez-Gaza wants to have her facial features altered and move to Albuquerque to become a flower shop owner through a witness protection program. There are certain islands where, for the right price, someone can remain anonymous for long periods of time. Then too, there are certain communes where nuns still wear full habits and do not communicate with the outside world. Ms. Menendez-Gaza successfully dressed as a man and slipped past hundreds of people who had just seen her on stage. She's also a very skillful actress. So she knows how to go instantly incognito. Bravo, by the way."

"Not my best effort at being in disguise. I forgot to remove my nail polish. I had to keep my jacket closed so no one would notice my breasts and my hands in my pants pockets until I got into the cab. Then when I paid the cab driver, he asked for my autograph."

"Nevertheless, lesson learned. My point being you know how to alter your appearance and change your voice when need be."

"I do, yes, but I do not want to have to live that way every day."

"Then it's settled, Angel. Will you be my plus one in name only for the foreseeable future?"

"Gregory, this could put you in danger and your reputation in jeopardy."

"If this hoax will help get to the bottom of this situation, I'm willing to risk it."

"Good," said Slade. "I know you're Catholic, Angelique, and it goes against the grain for you, but I suggest you two act as if you're living together here. Gregory, your brother has this place secured better than Fort Knox. Your windows are shatter resistant to gale force winds of up to 120 mph, but you also have automatic, electronic, hurricane shutters. The only vulnerable area is the rooftop when it's not closed in and locked down."

"You know this because ...?"

"I had a team running entry scenarios. Your walls are eighteen inches reinforced steel, concrete, and brick and block, so that's out. Usually the roof and underground are the simplest ways to penetrate a property relatively unnoticed. On your roof an assailant would literally have to skydive in. Underground you have a cistern and water filtration and purification systems. The moment there is a breach, an alarm would sound and if the assailants didn't know what to expect, they would likely drown.

"Alter your schedule somewhat. I'm betting a place this well-fortified in the middle of the city has an in-home gym."

"Beside the garage. About two thousand square feet."

"With a lady love on the premises, you'd likely not want to be up and out quite so early or often. Use your in-home gym or run at different or unpredictable times of the day or night. Accept as many of those invitations to appear somewhere as you can stomach. Be as unpredictable as possible.

"Angelique, you are never to go anywhere alone. You're going to have developed several new girlfriends. You'll shop, lunch, and play tennis or golf, but never alone. You're surrounded by your staff when you're at your restaurant. Two new chefs you hired will come on board this week. Don't worry. They actually are *bona fide,* board-certified cooks, but they both pack heat so to speak. If you're there in the restaurant, they are also. Even when you take days off to spend time with Gregory at some well-publicized event, they will be in the restaurant to deter any attempt to breach your security again. Your doorman and night watchman, Mr. Roy Conway, will have back up so he can come and go without fear of someone breaking in while he's away from the premises. That is true also for your doorman at the apartment building.

"Be aware of little things, like turning on or off various lights in the house. You're supposed to be lovers so synchronize your movements as much as possible. As we move deeper into the fall, lights can signal where you two are in the house to anyone who is keeping watch and we will be keeping watch twenty-four-seven. However, we will be using heat-signature equipment when necessary to ensure you're the only two people inside your home."

"How long do you think we will have to keep up this charade?"

"It's a good thing you're friends, because there is no way to predict how long it will take to wrap this up, but suffice-it-to-say this is among our highest priorities. With your full cooperation, we'll push for an expeditious conclusion."

Gregory and Angelique turned and looked at each other. He reached out his hand and she took it, lacing his fingers with hers. "Let's do it," he said, looking into her eyes.

She met his stare evenly and, with a small smile and an inclination of her head, nodded her agreement.

"Great," said Donald as he rose from the table. "You'll keep me informed," he said to Slade.

"Yes, sir," he agreed.

After a round of farewell hugs, everyone left except Aretha who planned to spend the night. She was a licensed pilot and would fly herself back to Boston in the morning.

Later that night, Angelique showered and dressed for bed in the room Aretha chose to sleep in. She wandered out of the bathroom and helped herself to the space on the bed opposite where Aretha sat against a mountain of pillows keying into her iPad.

"You're feeling antsy and unsettled, aren't you?" Aretha asked her best friend without a break in her rhythm on the keyboard. She was actually composing a piece of music for the piano.

"I am, yes," Angelique said, stretching out on the king-sized bed, her hands laced behind her head watching Aretha work.

"That's because you're in love with Gregory."

Angelique turned to her side facing Aretha, her head palmed in her left hand. "It seems like all of my young life I've had a crush on your brother. Do you remember when he was teaching me how to change the oil in a car?"

"I do, yes. We were in DC in the driveway at Benny's house in Georgetown." She didn't mention, even to Angelique, she had the ability of total recall. Her siblings did not know. She only shared her ability with her parents who were as anxious as she was to keep it a secret.

"That same weekend Gregory was trying to teach me and Joyce how to dance. He gave a party at the end of the summer at the house in

Georgetown so he could introduce Joyce to people he knew. He went to all that trouble so Joyce would have friends to pal around with while she attended college. One of the people Joyce met that day was Peter Callaway."

"I remember it too."

"See, that's what did it for me. Gregory always puts himself out to help people. He's not selfish or egotistical or arrogant. He's accomplished so much and he's really famous, but he's what he was when I was a kid. He's just Gregory.

"Make it an A sharp to change the tempo," she commented on Aretha's piece of music.

"That's a good suggestion. That takes me to the bridge."

"You're not just in love with my brother, you've also got a giant-sized amount of hero worship mixed in. I love and respect Gregory Clayton and he's all things good and wonderful in my view, but he's just a good guy. He doesn't see himself as anyone special, so don't make the mistake of putting him up on a pedestal."

"It's hard not to. You should see him with Dejon and Keaton. He's so natural with them. They respect him and for Mrs. Joyner he hung the sun."

"I have seen him with the boys. It's what's expected of us, Angelique. It's the first principle laid down by our ancestors. *We strive for and maintain unity in the family, in our communities, in our nation and in the human race.* That's how all of us, my parents, grandparents, aunt, uncles, cousins, and siblings were raised. So, you may think what he is doing with the Joyners is extraordinary, but really for any of us it's just the norm. It's what's expected."

"I know exactly how the Joyners feel because your family, particularly Vivian, did exactly the same thing for us when we came to America with nothing from Peru. My *momi* had to work at any job she could find all along the way from our village in Peru to Washington, DC, to find out what happened to my father. Within days of our arrival Vivian had us living in her home and taking care of us like we were her family. All of the housemates took care of us."

Aretha chuckled. "That's because you are family."

She smiled. "I guess I am and you, Ardon, Joyce, and Margo are my BFFs. All of you have made it abundantly clear in the past few days, but, Aretha, do you think Gregory will ever see me as anyone other than his family, his little sister?"

"I don't know the answer to that question, Angel. You're the sister of his heart, but whether you're the woman of his dreams is an entirely different question."

Chapter 9

It was approaching eight o'clock in the morning when Angelique heard the security chime Mrs. Joyner's name. The door opened then closed before she heard the older woman's feet on the stair treads. Aretha was up early and out to visit with Dejon and Keaton before they left for school and she left to fly back to Boston.

It was Wednesday morning of what Angelique considered her confinement. She wasn't angry about the efforts being made to keep her safe, but she was unaccustomed to being idle for such long periods of time.

New York was such a vibrant city she learned to set her daily pace to the energy the city life offered. She was usually up at the crack of dawn trudging through the wholesale markets selecting foods for her menu before other restaurant employees picked over the best choices of meats, fish, vegetables, and fruits. These last few days she could barely get her eyes open before eight. Even at that, the bed was so comfortable she had to fight her way from under the zillion-count covers.

Usually, Gregory was up and out for his morning run. Then he showered, dressed and was out the door for his walk to his office before seven. He said he got an early start to check the Asian and European markets so he could get a handle on what to expect the American markets would do during the day. He explained how an infestation of locusts in China would have an impact on rice imports for the short and long term, increasing the value of rice grown in other places around the world. The slightest and sometimes seemingly most insignificant or inconsequential thing could impact world markets in unusual, unexpected, and unpredictable ways. Gregory said his job was to study those events and determine when and how they might impact CTI's clientele or financial products. Just as mad cow disease in England caused the demand for American beef to skyrocket; it was all a case of supply and demand. The smaller the supply often meant the greater the demand. That explanation helped Angelique understand more clearly why Gregory took certain actions on behalf of his and CTI's clients. Knowledge of government bond issues was the same thing as needing to know the predictable behavior of the stock market.

With the new-found understanding of what Gregory, Margo, and Joyce did and why they did it, Angelique flipped on the flat screen in her bedroom and tuned to one of the business channels. She propped herself up in bed against the pillows, determined to learn more about Gregory's professional life, but, try as she might, the short-hand nomenclature confused her and the television program didn't hold her interest. She turned to a cooking show on the Gourmet Channel featuring a hot, handsome chef, Daryl Mason. He was young and virile and could hold the interest of any woman with a pulse.

Finally, she showered, dressed, and went down the stairs where she found Mrs. Joyner with her hands to her elbows in bread dough.

"Good mornin' ta' ya', Miss Angel."

"Good morning, Mrs. Joyner. How are you today?"

"Oh, just fine and dandy, I'd say. Well, except that dang, fool ex-husband of mine came banging at my door last night waking me up out of a good sleep. Claimed he was lonely and missing my good lovin'. He wanted to move back in with me and my grand boys and get married again. I'm sure he just sees how well we're getting on and he wants someone to take care of his rusty butt."

"Oh, my, what did you do?"

"Oh, I let him spend the night in my bed while he rocked my world. Then before he woke this morning, I called Mildred to come and get her husband," she said, and giggled. "Of course, I had another dose of him before Mildred got there."

Angelique just grinned and shook her head at Mrs. Joyner's glee.

"That old man has still got the moves, but after twenty-three years of marriage to him I don't need to ride that horse every day, if you get my meaning. Whenever I want him, I can just pucker up and whistle."

Angelique did understand though she had never experienced the rapture.

She wasn't one for matchmaking, but she wondered whether she should introduce Mrs. Joyner to her restaurant's doorman and security guard Roy Conway. They were around the same age, it seemed, and Mr. Conway, a former Marine, was very fit. He lost his wife more than ten years earlier to breast cancer and lived in a little efficiency behind the bar, while he works for her. His daughter, who never visits, and a brother he isn't close to who lived in Indiana are his only family. It might be an interesting connection for both of them, she thought.

Mrs. Joyner continued making the bread Gregory requested for his poker game and periodically checking his two pot roasts in the large, slow-cooker crockpots. Angelique prepared fresh vegetables: carrots, celery, and baby white potatoes to steam in a different slow cooker using the *au jus* from the roasts with thyme, oregano, and peppers. They sat over hot coffee and warm scones Angelique baked the day before and heated them while waiting for the bread to rise. Even the dough, one of onions and the other of garlic, smelled great, Angelique told Mrs. Joyner who shared her recipe. By the time the dough had risen twice, Mrs. Joyner had two, two-foot long loaves on large baking sheets ready to be buttered and popped into the oven.

A little after three-thirty in the afternoon, Gregory came home in sweats, his laptop in his briefcase hanging from his shoulder, dry cleaning over his arm and with Dejon and Keaton in tow. They greeted their grandmother and her in turn and then headed for the office space that had a library table. They spread their books and bags out and went to the kitchen bar for the snack with milk Mrs. Joyner poured into tumblers. Gregory headed up the stairs presumably to hang up his dry cleaning, take a shower and change clothes. When he returned, a half hour later, he wore jeans, tennis shoes, and a white T-shirt that looked fabulous hugging his body. He smelled of something masculine, but deliciously edible.

He clapped his hands. "All right, let's get started."

The boys picked up their snack debris, dumped it in the trash, and headed to the library table while Gregory went down to the lower level and brought back a cardboard box full of scrap pieces of lumber cut to resemble miniature two-by-fours. Apparently Dejon had a project requiring him to use math to demonstrate how a house is built. They rolled out a large sheet of paper and commenced designing a floor plan for the one-story house he had to build. Step-by-step Dejon worked writing down all of the measurements with Gregory and Keaton looking on or offering suggestions as he hot glued the project together. By six-thirty the project was completed and the miniature house was under roof. The smile on Dejon's face was priceless as he displayed the finished product. There were windows and doors appropriate to the size of the model. With the removable roof, the interior on display held three bedrooms and two baths looked suspiciously like the apartment they lived in. Dejon admitted he measured the rooms in the apartment where they lived and then shrunk them to use as a template for the model home. He had to figure out where to add a back door since his apartment didn't have one.

All in all, it was a credible effort and enterprising project with neatly typed notes. He was ready for Show-and-Tell on Friday. Dejon beamed his approval when Gregory asked whether he could come to the school to see his presentation to the class. Shortly thereafter, the boys and Mrs. Joyner left, leaving the project on the library table for safe keeping. Gregory would put the project in the back of his SUV and take the boys to school on Friday morning.

"He did a really fine job, Gregory," Angelique commented after the Joyners left.

"He did, yes. I think he has a real aptitude for design and construction. I'm going to find ways to cultivate his interest. My friend, Roderick Baylor, has a summer program for youth interested in the building and construction trades as a career. I'll talk with him to see whether Dejon might fit into the program. Keaton's questions about broadcasting or cablecasting are the first indications of something he may be interested in. If I send Dejon to DC, I'll have to find something interesting in the area for Keaton to do over the summer too. I'll speak with his teachers and see what they suggest. I'll also contact the cable company here in the city to see whether they have any summer programs for young people."

"I've met Roderick. He and his wife, JaiHonnah, are friends of Vivian's and they remodeled my restaurant and bar for me. In fact, JaiHonnah and Vivian were in undergrad together. That's a great idea. I have several at-risk youth-in-training at my restaurant. When this craziness is over, you are welcomed to bring him there to gauge his interest in food service."

"Thanks, I'll do it. If there is one thing the boy knows how to do really well, it's how to eat."

They laughed together, but they were sitting on one of the window seats facing each other, their knees touching. Gregory played with the end of Angelique's illustriously full, thick hair falling loosely around her shoulder and down her back. They had been sipping glasses of excellent red wine while talking.

Angelique shifted, cuddling into Gregory's right side. "This will end, won't it, Gregory? I mean, I will be able to go back to living a normal life again, right?"

He brushed a hand over her head on his shoulder and then gave her a comforting squeeze. He didn't know the answer to that question, but he wanted to keep her spirits up.

When he didn't answer immediately, she turned her head to look up at him, her mouth a breath away from his when he looked down into her eyes.

"Gregory?" she breathed the question.

The moment was pregnant with possibilities. She had only to lean up a fraction or two or for him to lean down before there was no space left between them. They stared searching each other's eyes and then the front doorbell rang breaking the spell and jolting them back from the brink.

Gregory immediately got up to answer the door, depositing his wine glass on a cocktail table on his way. Too much wine would make any man lose his grip on his behavior around a young woman as beautiful as Angelique. He refused to imbibe anymore tonight.

"*Wow!* Man, this is some place!" Jackson Chase enthused after Gregory answered the door. He offered Gregory a bottle of wine as he took off his top coat and hung it in a walk-around closet at the base of the steps.

"Thanks. I forgot you haven't been here before. I'll give you a tour later."

"I'd like that. I was surprised at how close you are to the office."

"I usually walk," he said, as they headed up the stairs.

"Man!" Jackson declared when they reached the top step. "Look at the space! You've got acres!"

"I need every inch when my family shows up," he said, laughing. "You remember my friend, Angelique, don't you?" he asked when Angelique approached and offered her hand.

It had taken her time to recover from the near mid-air collision of their mouths. Her nipples were hard peaks and need had settled between her thighs. Now she hoped her breathing had slowed and she was relaxed enough to pull off a casualness she was far from feeling.

"Yes, I do. Although you probably won't remember, I had the pleasure of eating at your restaurant months ago."

"Yes, of course, I remember. You were with Yvonne Kincaid, the stage actress, for the late night seating."

"You have some memory."

"Thank you. Would you like something to drink? I'm the unofficial hostess this evening."

"Then this is for you," he said, taking the wine back from Gregory and handing it to Angelique. "I'll have a glass of this."

"Coming up," she said, smiled, and walked away.

Gregory continued to show Jackson around the first level while Angelique decanted the wine to let it breathe before sampling it and pouring a glass for both Gregory and Jackson.

"You'll have to give me the name of your architect. This place is awesome."

"Sure, her name is JaiHonnah Baylor. She and her husband, Roderick, are a team at Baylor and Baylor Design and Developers. They have offices in Washington, DC. She designs and engineers and he does the development and construction end."

"JRock, the basketball star?" At Gregory's nod of agreement, he said, "I heard he was from north-east DC, but I didn't know he still lived there. That's convenient. My project is just outside of Washington, not far from Annapolis, Maryland."

"That shouldn't be a problem. They do projects worldwide."

While Gregory and Jackson continued their discussion and tour, Angelique got busy in the kitchen area making hot and cold *hors d'oeuvres* as Gregory's guests began to arrive. His space was perfect for this gathering of friends, about thirty in all. She set up buffet style on a kitchen trestle table and sideboard by a window. Gregory served beer and wine from a rollaway bar. She decorated with colorful napkins, fat, scented candles she found in a beautifully restored antique China cabinet, Kenneth's work she'd bet, and gathered pretty, colorful fall leaves from the rooftop deck and scattered them over the tabletop.

There were six round tables of five men and women equally spaced so there was plenty of room to move about without having to bump into anything or anyone. As the players lost all of their chips, they fell out of the game leaving only the winners to continue to do battle. By midnight there was only one table of five poker players left. Jackson Chase, China McAllister, and Margo Chandler were three of the five still fighting it out. In the end they counted their winnings and China was victorious with the biggest pile of pennies to her credit.

By one in the morning, almost all of the food was gone as well as all of the guests and the space put to right again. Gregory was folding the last of the six tables to return them to storage on the garage level of his home.

"Thanks, Angelique, you were a huge help tonight. Your canopies and *hors d'oeuvres* were a big hit," he said. He stuffed his hands in his pockets to keep them off of her. Their encounter earlier in the evening was a close call. He didn't like his chances of keeping his hands to himself if he showed her the affection he felt for her.

Was Aretha right? she wondered. Was what she felt for Gregory real love or hero worship? After all, what did she know about love? Of course, she felt the sensation for her family and friends; even for her fans. Yet, she had never loved a boy or a man. She never let herself fall much. Certainly not to the point Mrs. Joyner felt for her Melvin. Angelique didn't think she could love a man piece-meal. With her, it was all or nothing. Those new feelings would have to be given more thought. She didn't want to start something only to realize what she felt for Gregory was only a latent school-girl crush. She also didn't want to lose the closeness they shared for many years just because she was curious. She didn't know how these things worked, but she would find out.

She would ask her friend Joyce.

She had a certain look in her eyes that made him want to take a giant mental step back and pull her into his arms simultaneously. The look of a full-grown woman with the body of a dewy, soft youngster. That image kept getting tangled in his head. He wanted to protect her and to make instantaneously, unbridled love to her. The dichotomy was enough to drive a sane man over the brink.

Slade told him to pretend to be in an intimate relationship with Angelique. The problem was he felt like he wanted to make the relationship real in every sense of the word.

Chapter 10

The next morning, as Angelique ambled down the stairs to the kitchen to make something to eat, she heard what sounded like an engine misfiring in the garage. That was unusual because, under most circumstances, the house was devoid of noise. She assumed she was alone in the house since Gregory was generally up and out early.

She continued halfway down the stairs toward the front door and looked to her right through the wide, squat, transom windows into the garage. There she saw Gregory toward the rear of the space working under the hood of an old car. She continued down the stairs and opened the door to the garage. The sensational sound of the singing group Ivy was belting out soulful lyrics from their new CD and Gregory was singing along as he worked.

Just as she approached, Gregory's head came up out from under the hood and turned in her direction. His penetrating eyes locked onto hers with a steady gaze. She felt her blood swimming faster through her body and a tingle crawling up her spine. Even when he ducked his head to swipe perspiration from his face onto the shoulder of his black T-shirt, the movement was somehow sexy, she thought. Still his eyes never left hers. Leaning up, his hands were braced on a cloth covering the left, front fender. "Did I wake you?" he asked while wiping his hands on another cloth and then shutting off the music with a remote control device he retrieved from the roof of the car.

She watched, transfixed, as his muscles flexed with the simple movements. "No, I can't hear any noise transfer in this house up on that level."

"Good soundproofing. Are you hungry? I could make something . . ." he trailed off and grinned at her sardonic expression.

"*Seriously?* You do know I'm a trained and certified Le Cordon Bleu chef, right? I did prove it last night, didn't I?"

He chuckled. "Rumor has it, but then you can't believe everything you hear, now can you?" he joked. "Rumor has it you had my first baby at age eight."

"This is true. I must have been a late bloomer," she parried. "What are you doing?"

"Oh, uh, this?" he stumbled, momentarily entranced by her absolute sexy, early-morning smile. Her eyes were still dewy, her face creamy and devoid of makeup. "I'm restoring this car as a gift for my parents' anniversary."

"Looks like it needs a paint job," she commented as she walked around it and over the hose attached to the exhaust pipe that transferred the fumes to the outside.

"It does, yes. Once I get everything properly fitted and up and running, I'll send the frame out to a fabricator I use in Jersey for an electrostatic bath."

"That's a paint job, right?"

"Of sorts, yes. The fabricator scrapes any rust and immerses the chassis into a tank bath and shoots... Never mind," he said, and laughed when she purposely crossed her eyes and took on a glazed, Prozac look.

She turned her head, looking around to keep from salivating over his broad, firm chest in a well-used, black, Million Man March T-shirt, his narrow waist, and old cut-off jeans with stress patches in interesting places. He wore a ratty, old pair of tennis shoes with no socks. "What's in there?" she asked, pointing to a closed door.

He scrubbed his hands up to his elbows in a deep sink and dried them at the rear of the garage. "Come, I'll show you. We never did finish the house tour."

She followed him through a door leading into a long hallway. As they entered, lights popped on illuminating the space. The first door on the right opened into a well-stocked, brick wine cellar with tables, tasting bar, and stools. She wandered from row to row to row pulling out bottles at random and inspecting the labels. She wasn't as knowledgeable as her sommelier, but in her estimation, Gregory had some really good to excellent selections. Suddenly all of the bottles shifted slightly. She jolted and looked up quizzically at Gregory.

"It's automated so the contents don't develop sediment. The bottles are turned about every thirty minutes."

"There are at least three or four thousand bottles in here."

"Actually more than that. Imagine if I had to turn them by hand every thirty minutes. I wouldn't have time to do anything else."

"Why so many? You couldn't possible drink all of this."

"It's an investment." He told her about individual bottles of wine and various wine cellars which sold at auction at Christie's for obscene amounts of money. He bought cases of wine from a sommelier, Merissa Talbert, whom he once dated and still did periodically if they were both unattached. She always kept in touch and got great deals for him when she found wine cellars for sale. If they were both between relationships they might combine business with a little pleasure and go tour wineries for a few days or a week. He was negotiating to buy an old wine cellar she recommended in the Netherlands. He wasn't sure of the vintages because he couldn't break away to go visit the cellar with her as he planned before this trouble came up involving Angel. Nevertheless, he was going ahead with the acquisition sight unseen on Merissa's recommendation alone.

With one last look, he turned off the light and led Angelique across the hall through another door where the lights were already on. There, rows upon rows of fresh vegetables and fruits grew in bubbling and churning troughs of water.

"A hydroponics farm?" she asked, amazed.

"A small one as compared to the ones my family owns in Summer County."

There were heads of lettuce, cabbage, spinach, squash, green beans, lima beans, carrots, tomatoes, onions, red, green and yellow bell peppers, hot peppers, white and sweet potatoes, cucumbers, kale, turnip greens and collards in sections apart from vinery fruits like strawberries, raspberries, blue and black berries, and red, white, green and purple grapes. She remembered him mentioning to Mrs. Joyner he had to harvest vegetables for his pot roasts, but she had no idea he had all of this in house. No wonder everything tastes so fresh. He had an awesome array of fresh herbs in his garden.

"I never thought of doing this," Angelique said, awe-inspired. "This is wonderful."

"Help yourself," he said, pulling a few grapes from the vine to pop in his mouth.

She followed suit and the sparkle in her eyes revealed her pleasure at the sweet taste. "This is delicious."

"They're pretty ripe. Here, look at this," he said, cutting a bunch of green grapes from another vine. He headed to an old-fashioned, table-top-mounted press. Inserting the grapes he cranked the handle. Juice flowed into a ceramic bowl. Discarding the remnants into a garbage disposal, he then poured the juice through a strainer into a clear glass measuring cup to check clarity. From there he took two chilled glasses from a refrigerator and poured equals shares into each. Together they sampled the juice.

"Low acidity," Angelique commented. "White grape juice."

"Yes, but I am experimenting with making wine," he said, putting all of the things they used into a dishwasher and setting it to start. Once done, he led her through another door where small, ten-gallon, wooden barrels lay side-by-side on shelves with flow taps on one end. "I'm doing okay with the pomegranate wine, but I'm a bust with trying to create a strawberry wine. If I can keep Dejon and Keaton from eating all the products, I may end up with a nice strawberry preserve or some great raisins from the grapes."

"They're fresh fruit fanatics, I've noticed."

"They come in here and raid the fruit to make frappe. It's the closest they can get to a milk shake. Every blue moon I'll make ice cream in an old churn I have down here; particularly if mom sends a crate of pecans to me. I inhale pecans and the boys like them grated with fresh fruit on their cereal."

"Now I see where they get it from."

He shrugged. "I grew up on a hydroponics farm," he said, laughing. "Have you seen the one on Chuck's and Vivian's farm? It's massive."

"I have, yes, and you're right, but they also have a fishery."

"I've thought about it, but a fishery would eat up too much space. They have plenty of space and have a lot more mouths to feed than I do," he said, and laughed as he led her back into the hall. The storeroom was a room that could have been a small convenience store. It contained dry goods as well as bushels of corn, apples, oranges, and other things in a cool, dry environment. Then there were the clear glass refrigerator units stocked with meats, fish, and poultry. Clear bags of frozen vegetables were labeled with the date each was harvested and stored. Still more glass jars contained large quantities of fruits and vegetables canned in natural juices. Another door led to a fully-equipped gym.

Angelique just stood and stared. A reader board was at the top of what was likely a twenty-foot-high ceiling. It had to be, she surmised, to allow long, tall, fire trucks and other emergency vehicles to be garaged in this space. Below it on the wall was an array of flat screens which could be viewed from any point in the room. Looking at it now, it was hard to imagine this space as one where firemen lived and worked for decades. Now it was fitted out as a single family home, albeit four-level, mansion-sized in what used to be The Bowery, formerly the dregs of the city.

She wandered around each piece of equipment and looked up at the basketball hoop on a half-court expanse. Clearly, Gregory was serious about taking care of his body and the results stood out in proud relief. She liked to work out too. She wasn't wearing her gear, but promised herself she would visit his gym later in the day. Now that she knew he had fresh fruit and vegetable gardens, she would be back to harvest vegetables for lunch and dinner.

"Is there anything else down here? A golf course or something?" she teased.

"My nieces and nephews want a bowling alley, but I begged off because I would have to give up my basketball court to accommodate their wishes. So that's pretty much it, except for the storage and utility rooms," he said, leading her to another door off the hallway. "I operate on a geothermal system primarily for power coupled with the rooftop photovoltaic arrays which include mainstream materials like monocrystalline silicon, polycrystalline silicon, amorphous silicon, cadmium telluride, and copper indium gallium selenide/sulfide. Of course, on days like today when it's overcast and raining, the house operates on geothermal with a propane back up. It's all automated through smart-house technology. I have access from my smart phone or computer no matter where I am. The water filtration and purification systems will be going all day collecting and cleaning the rain water draining from the roof. Some I use for the hydroponics, but the rest is for flushing toilets, washing clothes, and bathing or a final purification for potable water for cooking and drinking."

He showed the equipment to her and explained how it worked, but her eyes kept dropping to his mouth while he talked.

"Oh, hell," he groaned and brought her flush against his needful body. Everything about her screamed provocative messages to his brain while his mating instincts took over. He caught her off guard, but then she responded with absolute and unapologetic abandon.

He ravished her mouth or she ravished his, his brain was too fuzzy at that point from the heady taste of her to distinguish who did what to whom. With his strength diminishing, he managed to set her away from him, yet his forehead and hers still connected while he fought to get air into his lungs.

"I apologize for that. I should not have kissed you."

"Apology not accepted. I wanted that kiss and much, much more. You are not dense, Gregory. You had to know what I want."

"I know this is not right. You're younger than my sister, your best friend, and you're in trouble on more than one level. We've been thrown together for a period of time. It's just infatuation you feel and it will fade in time when this is over."

"Exactly what is it you feel? What emotion made you kiss me?"

"Lust," he admitted, "but you're too young for me."

"I'm soon-to-be twenty-one, Greg!" she said, vehemently. "I'm not a baby! This is virgin territory for me, I'll admit, but I'm not stupid, naive or immature. I know when a man has a look of desire in his eyes and I've seen the look in your eyes for me."

"'Virgin territory?' Have you had sex before?" Her innocence was as blatant as neon lights on Broadway. "Oh, hell, Angel," he moaned. "The way I touched you—."

"Is exactly what I want . . . need for you to do to me, Greg. I want to know what it feels like to have a man . . . to have you make love with me for the first time."

"You've waited this long, Angel. It may be old-fashioned for some, but not for you. Wait for the man who will love you for the rest of your life and his."

"That man can't be you because why?"

He took a deep breath, closed his eyes and shook his head. "Let's not go down that road. Right now we have to focus on your security and your business."

She wanted to argue, but feared losing the closeness they shared if she pressed the issue now. Instead, she rose on her toes and planted a warm, lingering kiss on his mouth. "I'll make breakfast," she said, and left him standing in the utility room.

The weighty silence was broken when the rainwater gushed into the cistern. Why the hell had he given in to his desire to touch her? He was not the type of man to take advantage of a younger woman, especially not one he had watched grow up from gangly limbs, knobby knees, and pigtails to fill out in all the right places to become a super model. He wasn't some randy teenager out to score with a super-hot chick. That was his sister's best friend, Angelique, who he nearly ravished in the freakin' utility room! She deserved the beauty of her first experience to be on her wedding night with romantic candle-light and music. He was not going to begin thinking of that scene or of her as a woman.

After breakfast, Gregory went to hibernate with his work as if he were in his office blocks away. Slade suggested they make it appear they were lovers spending quality time together when, in fact, Angelique was in the kitchen space concentrating on writing her first cookbook. At some points she would leave samples of her experiments for him to sample. She would go up to his rooftop herb garden or down to the garage level for fruits or vegetables. For lunch she made an interesting beef stew with cubes of leftover pot roast in a thick, brown-broth gravy with carrots, celery, white potatoes, green peas, garlic and onions all out of his hydroponics garden. With hunks of onion bread he sopped up the last of the gravy in his bowl without taking his eyes off of a potential gem he found in the textile stocks for a midsized company.

He had been watching the progress of this particular entity over time and liked what he saw. He investigated the backgrounds of the principals and their highly-placed officers and staff members. It was a well-run company with dedicated employees and a low turnover rate. They were looking for investors to expand because they received a contract to outfit a fleet of aircraft and cruise ships owned and operated by Christoval Oleg 'Ollie' Ossian Aristotle, a Greek shipping tycoon. Greg remembered getting to know the man fairly well because he briefly dated one of Ollie's daughters, Anastasia. Ollie often dated his Aunt Mariah, the French Mariah, star of the European entertainment industry and songstress extraordinaire. He also knew Ollie to be a sound businessman and believed, if he placed the contract with this US-based textile company, he was expecting excellent results. Sometimes it was not only *what* he knew, but also *who* he knew which made the difference on whether or not he took a chance on a long shot or made an investment viable. He put in a call to Ollie and then to the CEO of the textile company and made his day. That investment would pay off handsomely with a couple of million in the short term. He also bought into the company and onto its board of directors.

There were a few more deals he did before he came up for air at the closing bell on the Exchange. He worked up his tally sheet for the day and filed it for Joyce's review. Shortly thereafter her face popped up in a block on one of his computer screens.

"Whoa, Boy Wonder, you were zoning today!"

He laughed. "I got a late start, but the market was fast and loose, just the way I like it."

"Yeah, thanks for the heads-up about the cold snap in Idaho. It probably means we'll be importing potatoes for chips from outside the US market in the spring."

"Likely, yes. The weather predictions didn't anticipate snow this early in Idaho. Farmers can't plow their fields to harvest their crops until the snow melts and the ground thaws. If this early snowstorm keeps up it means they'll lose their yield this season."

"They'll lay off workers so there will be a mild down-turn in their local area economy for the foreseeable future."

"They will and it will affect the local municipalities' and counties' tax base. Two counties have bond initiatives out for road and bridge improvements and repairs. Three companies are vying for those projects and have accepted the RFPs. I see an opportunity for CTI to go in with a low-percentage bond loan so the counties can meet their obligations."

"I saw it in your analysis. If the weather conditions don't improve then those companies won't be in a position to hire the potato farm workers displaced by the early heavy weather and meet their deadlines under their contracts for other projects. I agree with you. Because this will require a substantial outlay of capital, let's put it for vote on tomorrow's agenda."

"Agreed. A lot of those are still mom-and-pop family farms which have been held together for generations just like my family's farm. We should underwrite their losses this season for a return next year. This could mean the difference between survival and having to sell to the large conglomerate corporate farm owners and manufacturers."

"Does your family worry about it for their farm business?"

"Not so much, no. My uncle Romello Dixon and his son, James, head Alexander-Dixon Industries (ADI), our family owned and operated company. James has doctorates in animal husbandry and new technology farming. Uncle Romello has an MBA. They keep up with cutting-edge farming techniques and because we're an O and O entity, we diversified and cut out the middle man as much as possible. That way we have better control of the pricing for our goods in the marketplace. It makes us more competitive. My storeroom is full of ADI products. We not only produce the products, we also can the produce and ship directly to the retail outlets. The majority of Angelique's menu comes directly from ADIs farm produce to the table in twenty-four hours or less. That's true for all of ADI's customers. We have an on-line whole foods arm which is very active.

"The weather can impact delivery, but not production. Since we're a hydroponics operation, we operate twenty-four-seven year round. We use recycled glass, medal and rubber for producing shatter-resistant containers as another arm of ADI's operation. Hell, we still bottle milk from our cows and the milk man delivers in Summer County in a milk wagon," he said, laughing. "There's something to be said for doing it the old-fashioned way."

Joyce laughed too. "My dad still does it the old-fashioned way, too, on our farm in Pennsylvania. So does the Jackson family. Though we don't have as many livestock as we used to, we still bale hay and straw and sell it to the other farmers and to the glass manufacturing operation in our county."

"Every one of my siblings is doing something other than farming. At least your brothers, sisters and their families are around to help your dad and Mrs. Jackson on the farm."

"For the most part, yes, but, of course, they've all got their own businesses in the building trades."

"Everyone except you and Chuck."

She laughed. "Even we're expected to gather eggs when we go home to visit."

"Me, too."

"Before I let you go, how is our girl?"

"She made crepes with fresh fruit compote for breakfast, beef stew from last night's leftovers for lunch, and I think I smell roasted Cornish hens stuffed with wild rice and a vegetable medley for dinner. In between, she worked on her cookbook and made samples of her recipes. What does it tell you?"

"That she's keeping busy. It's a good thing. I'll make time over the weekend to visit."

"Call first. We'll be out and about quite a bit. We're at a music album release party later tonight for one of Jason Goins' acts, theatre awards show tomorrow night, and I'm working the color commentary on Saturday after my Little League's final game. Then I'm doing a cameo on Saturday Night Live. On Sunday we're at St. Marks for morning Mass then brunch at the Top of the Sixes."

"Wow! Hang in there, pal," she said, and was gone.

"Hanging," he said to himself, "by a thin thread," as he momentarily watched Angelique moving around in his kitchen.

Chapter 11

"Satin," the woman said, as she extended her hand to Gregory at his front door early on Monday morning. She took out her identification and handed it to him for inspection. Her companion did the same.

"Mata Hari," she said, offering her hand as well.

The code names were right and matched the pictures and profiles Slade provided for him and Angelique last week when he was in town for their initial meeting. Both women were lookers, but very different. Satin was around his age, Gregory guessed, if not a year or two younger, but Mata Hari had to be in her late thirties to mid-forties. Both women had an edge about them; an alertness to every slight change in the atmosphere of their surroundings. They scanned the space quickly, scoping out every detail, he'd bet.

"Please come in and have a seat. Would you like something to eat or drink?"

"Coffee, if it's not too much trouble."

"No trouble at all. This way," he said, leading them to the Keurig on the coffee bar and the array of coffee and tea options in a carousel. "I'll see whether Angelique is awake," he said, and headed up the steps.

He entered the bedroom where she slept and sat on the side of the bed to wake her. He was glad the light filtering into the room from the hall was low because it didn't appear, from her exposed shoulders, she was wearing anything to sleep in.

He woke her as gently as possible.

Her eyes opened and she smiled at him. She levered up and put her arms around him, claiming his mouth in a soul-shuddering kiss. The cover fell to her waist. He probably could have evaded her approach, but didn't. He refused to examine why.

There was nothing he wanted more than to crawl into bed with her and bury himself deep inside her. He let the kiss play out with her still warm, soft body under his hands.

"Good morning," she said, and laid her head on his shoulder. "I was dreaming about you when you woke me."

"It's time to get up, Angel. Slade Richardson's agents are here."

"So soon?"

"Yes," he said, rising from her side and kissing her forehead. "I'm heading out for my run. I'll see you when I get back." He was out the door as quickly as possible to avoid seeing her nude. He informed the agents Angelique would join them shortly; made sure they were settled with coffee and fat blueberry muffins Angelique baked the day before; and hit the door as if he were running for his life. He cued up Walter Mosley's most recent Easy Rawlins' mystery, inserted the earbuds, and started out at an easy pace without warming up. The kiss Angelique planted on him had his blood warm enough.

Freshly showered and dressed, her hair still a bit damp, Angelique made her way down the stairs and into the kitchen area. The agents both stood, showed their credentials to her, and extended their hands.

"It's a pleasure to meet you, Ms. Menendez-Gaza," the older one said, her face and voice somehow familiar.

"Thank you. Have we met before? You seem familiar."

"No, we haven't. This is your new best friend. You will introduce her as Leslie Grant if you need to in public," she said, smoothly, but thought she would have to have Slade switch her for a different agent. She couldn't think of any obvious connection between herself and Angelique, but it was another area she would have to ask Slade to explore. She couldn't afford to have her under-cover identify blown. "Why don't we sit? We have a lot to cover in this initial session."

In the hour or so since they began, Gregory returned from his run, dressed, and left for work. A car arrived and the agents took Angelique to her spa for her regular appointments for facial, mani-pedi, massage, and hair services. By two in the afternoon they were easy with each other, having had lunch at a popular uptown restaurant and shopping until four. They entered Angelique's bar, The Run Way, to wait for Gregory to join them for Happy Hour. Her employees were thrilled to see her, but were busy gearing up for the five o'clock seating.

It wasn't supposed to be possible for Angelique to look more beautiful than she usually did, Gregory thought, but she was absolutely radiant. In a bar full of people, at least half of whom were attractive women, she stood out even in a dimly lit room. She wore a deep maroon-colored sequenced swing dress which stopped just above her knees leaving her gorgeous legs free to be viewed and admired in maroon-colored, high-heeled, ankle boots.

When he entered the bar with Jackson Chase and Troy Jackson and removed his top coat, she stood to greet them with her companions. Then she laid a lip lock on him nearly eclipsing the flash of camera lights going off around them. It took moments for him to stabilize his breathing while he gazed into her mesmerizing eyes. The glass of wine helped, but she draped herself on him with her left arm around his shoulders and her right hand palming his right knee. He knew she was playing her role for the cameras and the crowd as they sipped wine and chatted with the group at large, signed autographs for and took pictures with club patrons, but her closeness, whispers in his ear, and natural scent were wreaking havoc on his psyche.

Fortunately, they all got up and went into dinner for the five o'clock seating. They continued their easy conversation, Jackson and Troy none the wiser the women they were introduced to were security agents assigned for Angelique's protection. After dinner, Angelique complimented her chef so profusely it brought tears to the man's eyes. The group left her restaurant and went dancing at some of the most popular night spots in the city. They made sure they were seen and photographed together at each location. It was past midnight when the car pulled away after depositing them on Gregory's doorstep.

"Tired?" he asked, as he and Angelique slowly climbed the stairs hand-in-hand from the vestibule to the first level of his home.

"No, not at all. I should be after a full day of activities and dancing tonight. You know, I had forgotten what a great dancer you are."

He chuckled at that as he took off his coat and loosened his tie. He helped her out of her coat matching her dress. "Thanks, but I was just trying to keep up and not make a complete fool of myself. Would you like something?"

"Water. I feel a little dehydrated."

"Coming up," he said, as he filled two glasses with ice and cold water before sitting beside her on the window seat. It seemed to be her favorite spot in his home filled with seating. He leaned back and stretched his left arm out behind her back, toed off his shoes and got comfortable while he drank his water. She leaned back in his arm, her back to his chest as she looked out of the window at the bridges and the lights from boats on the water.

"You know, I've never done one of those boat rides around the island."

"Then we'll have to put it on our itinerary. You want the day or night cruise?"

"Night, I think. That's when it all seems so magical. Did you have fun tonight?"

"I did, yes. We've had a busy time over the recent past."

"We have, haven't we? It's hard to believe all of this started a week ago Sunday. I've virtually moved in, caused you to break up with your girlfriend, and alter your life to fit mine."

"I enjoy having you here, Angel, especially when you feed me so much better than I can feed myself. And don't blame yourself for what happened between me and Alondra. She was not my 'girlfriend' in the conventional sense. We were more like friends with benefits. I've offered to continue our friendship, but it's her call on whether she chooses to accept. My life is finally mine to live as I want. I don't have a basketball schedule to contend with. I have a new career I enjoy, but it doesn't define who and what I am. I don't need to work to make ends meet, but it gives me a satisfying sense of accomplishment to be in a position to help a new business get off the ground or an existing business expand and add more people to the employment rolls. This country has got to get as close to full employment as possible if we're ever going to make a dent in the crime rate, poverty, our ability to improve education, cure homelessness, and a sense of helplessness. We've got to improve the justice system and find ways for nonviolent offenders to live productive lives once released from prison. Those things are more important to me now rather than whether a single relationship is successful."

"Well said, son," came the voice of Bernard Alexander, Gregory's father as he descended the stairs. He was followed by his wife of forty-plus years, Sylvia, and her sister, Mariah Benson.

"Dad? Mom? Aunt Mariah?" Gregory joyfully said, all vestiges of fatigue gone as he untangled himself from Angelique and rushed to his parents. He took each one in his arms and squeezed. "I didn't expect you until tomorrow. How are Satarah and the new baby?"

"It is tomorrow and they're both doing well," answered his aunt about her daughter and new granddaughter.

His parents had already gathered up Angelique in bear hugs and had her sitting between them on the window seat he had just vacated. After his aunt hugged her, he settled her in one of the, high-backed, wing chairs facing his parents and Angelique. He sat in a matching chair at his aunt's side.

"So you're doing all right?" Bernard asked of Angelique.

"Yes, sir. I'm fine. Everyone has been so kind to me, especially Gregory. If it wasn't for him, I never would have known what was going on."

"We are glad he can help you because we want you safe," said Sylvia. "I spoke with your parents and told them we were coming here to see you. They were so concerned we moved up the date of our visit. I think knowing we would be here with you helped settle them some."

"Gregory, you really need to call and talk with them, too," Bernard suggested.

"I'll do it. I don't know why I didn't think to do it before."

"Probably because you've been spending so much time seeing to every little detail to keep me safe and sane."

He looked into her heart-melting eyes and didn't notice the knowing expressions passing between his parents and aunt.

"So tell us about the newest Johnson," Gregory asked of his aunt.

"Katherine Lynn Johnson weighed in at a healthy but whopping eight pounds, seven ounces and twenty-inches long."

"I read that much on Aretha's blog along with seeing her pictures. How many fights did you have to break up between her four big brothers to see who would get to hold her first?"

"None. Her father hasn't let her or her two-year old sister out of his arms long enough for anyone except me to get their hands on her. We can barely get Douglas out of the house these days to go fight fires if his girls are awake. He's the fire chief, but it's a good thing he has an excellent group of firefighters working for him. He takes his paternity leave seriously. The boys have to drag him away to coach his Little League team."

"Six children. That's got to be hard on Satarah when she's operating her bed and breakfast."

"She's got good, competent help from the Ambassador's middle son, Miles Logan, who is learning to manage the facility. She focuses on cooking the meals. If you want to get out of the city, Angelique, you're welcomed to go visit The Summer House for as long as you like or at least until this threat to your safety is solved. It certainly would be warmer there than it is here in New York."

"I'll bring Angelique home for Thanksgiving, Aunt Mariah. We'll probably come down early and stay a while. Will you be home this year?"

"Probably. I plan to stay through New Year's."

"That's wonderful," Angelique said, a little breathless and shaken because Gregory intended to take her home with him for the holidays. She didn't want to get her hopes up, but it was Alexander family tradition the offspring brought home to meet the family only the person he or she intended to marry. Of course, she was no stranger to his relatives and she had been to Summer County before with her brother, Miguel, as Vivian's and Aretha's guests.

"It is," said Bernard. "Satarah wants to host the family Thanksgiving dinner at The Summer House this year."

"The family is getting so large now we need the extra space The Summer House offers. Your parents will be home by then, Angelique, and maybe Miguel will be finished with his movie or can make time to join us."

"I'll ask him after I speak with Anna and Fenster tomorrow," said Gregory. "How long can you stay in the city, Aunt Mariah?"

"I have some studio work to do here in New York which, if my voice cooperates in this cold weather, may take up to a week to complete. Then I'm headed back to Paris."

"You're releasing a new album?"

"Next year, perhaps, but no, this is for a movie score. I'm working with Jason Goins."

"I know him. One of my partners, China McAllister and he are dating. We were just at an album release party of one of his groups."

"Does China have a brother named Paris?"

"I think so. I've seen family pictures on her desk in the office."

"I believe I've met her parents. They're both military doctors."

"I think you're right. She has a younger sister Capri." He didn't mention China played matchmaker and hooked him up with her sister. Come to think of it, now that he was retired from professional sports, maybe he should rekindle the relationship with Capri once this ordeal was over so he could dislodge Angelique from his mind. At least as far as he recalled Capri McAllister was closer to his age and not a virgin.

"There are truly only six degrees of separation or less between people on this planet."

"We can pick this conversation up later in the morning," said Bernard as he rose from the window seat.

"You're right, dad. It's late."

Everyone hugged and headed up the stairs except Gregory and his father.

Gregory reset the house alarm and turned out most of the lights, leaving ambient lighting on for his family should any of them get up during the night.

"How bad is it really, son?"

"Pretty bad, dad. Kenneth moved quickly to secure her safety and I've reworked her business to make it easier for her to operate. I've taught her how to handle the accounting entries in an electronic program, but I'll keep my eyes on her progress for a while yet. Since CTI will be handling her investments going forward, I'm putting one of my firm's accountants on her business plan."

"Your mother and I are very proud of you, son."

"Thanks. I appreciate it."

"Is there something else you want to tell us?"

"No, not yet. I've always been able to talk with you and mom about everything and anything going on in my life, and it will never change. I'm working my way through my feelings, but I keep getting tangled up with the fact she's so young."

"I understand your reticence because she hasn't had much experience."

"None, dad. She hasn't had any experience. I don't want to move to another level in a relationship with her and then find out she isn't mature enough yet to know her own mind, let alone have other relations to compare ours with. I want a one-and-done with her, but I don't know whether she's ready for that yet."

"Maybe you'll be able to evaluate the possibility over the next few weeks with her in your home."

"She fits, dad. I know it already. She fits with our family and my friends. She has extraordinary beauty both inside and out. I see how she interacts so easily with Dejon and Keaton and I know she'll be a wonderful mother. She has warmth, a naked honesty I admire, and boundless love, yet she's so innocent. I can't help but love her for all things she is, but it's not enough to risk a lifetime on. I want to be deeply *in love* with a woman and feel the same depth of emotion in return. I want a forever kind of love like what you and mom have, like Kenneth and JeNelle, Benny and Stacy, Vivian and Chuck, Don and Cecile, James and Janice. Like what my grandparents and great-grandparents had. I won't settle for anything less."

"Your mama was barely twenty-one when we married. I was twenty-four and just finishing grad school. She was fresh out of nursing school, but I didn't want to lose her regardless of her age. I understand your concerns. So wait until you're sure it's what Angelique can offer you and you can offer her because, despite everything else, son, age ain't nothing but a number."

Chapter 12

"Hey, Greg."

"Peter? Hey, man, how's it going down under?"

"I'm not here in my head. Joyce is about to kick me to the curb. I'm trying like hell to get there before I lose the only woman I love."

"Now you're talking! So when will you be in town?"

"I don't know. I can't get a flight out of here for love nor money. I need your help. Do you think I can catch a hop on one of the Adventurer Executive—?"

"Hold one," Gregory interrupted and keyed up the existing flight schedules to see whether there was a jet anywhere near Peter in Australia. It was useful his sister, Vivian, owned the private airline, Adventurer Executive Air (AEA). Fortunately, there was an Irish rock band scheduled to leave Australia for a non-stop, chartered flight to Ireland. He booked Peter on the flight. Then from Ireland the flight was booked to return several top executives to Boston and New York. With any luck Peter would be back on US soil in twenty-four hours. "I've got you on a flight out of there in three hours. You'll be on your way to Ireland, but the flight schedule will have you back here in country after that."

"You're the best! Don't tell Joyce I'm coming. I want to surprise her, but I'm calling her family and mine. I'm going to marry my lady during Christmas and I want you to be my best man."

"You've got it, pal! I'll ask Angelique to help. When and where do you want to do this?"

"Her family is larger than mine. So I'm going to ask my family to come from Tennessee to Pennsylvania so we can do this in Monroe County at Joyce's home."

"And the honeymoon?"

"I don't have a clue. All I know is I want her to be my wife."

"Share what you're doing in Australia with her. Let her see what yachting means to you. Besides, it's warm there this time of year and Australia has some beautiful beaches. As my wedding gift to you two, I'll put a jet at your disposal to take you back there after the wedding for as long as you want to stay."

The weighty silence, Greg recognized, was Peter's attempt to control his emotions.

"You're the best . . ." he choked. "You're the best damn friend anyone could ever have," he said, sincerely, emotion still evident in his voice. "I'm naming my first born after you."

Greg chuckled. "Let's hope it's a boy. I don't think a girl would appreciate being called Gregory Clayton."

"I could always name her Alexis or Alexandra," Peter parried. "Alexandra Calloway sounds like a winner and appropriate because you're my best friend . . . you and Joyce that is," he said, laughing.

They talked a while longer while Peter packed before they hung up. Gregory checked on the location of a McCoy Hotel resort in proximity to where Peter lived in Australia. He booked the penthouse suite as an extra surprise wedding gift from him and Angelique for their friends. Hell, he was already thinking of himself and Angelique in terms of being a couple. He briskly rubbed his face, shook his head, and dismissed the bothersome thought. He'd discuss the gift with her at dinner tonight. For a change they didn't have any scheduled events to attend. His parents left with his aunt early in the morning after they had breakfast together, so it would be just the two of them alone tonight.

It was great having his parents and aunt in town for the week. They managed to go swimming in his pool every morning before breakfast for exercise. His parents and aunt were in great physical shape and healthy. Angelique enjoyed being a part of their daily activity. They managed to get out and about enjoying a multitude of activities, including an evening at Angelique's bar and restaurant. People recognized his aunt, the French Mariah, and encouraged her into singing a few of her top hits. He, his aunt, and Angelique were delayed in a long line of people waiting for pictures and autographs from them.

He took a deep, cleansing breath. He hoped he had the intestinal fortitude it would take to continue to keep his hands off of Angelique.

"Greg?" his Executive Assistant hailed from his office door.

"Yes?"

"Are you going to the gym today?"

"I am, yes, why?"

"Then you'd better get a move on or you're going to be late. Troy and Jackson are on their way to your office."

He looked at his watch. She was right. The day was flying by and he needed to expend his energy before he went home to Angelique.

"Hey, man, let's hat," called Troy with Jackson at his back.

"On it," Greg said, and grabbed his duffle, slung it over his left shoulder, and headed through the door toward the elevator while talking with his partners about the day's volatile market. A hired car waited for them at the front of the building. It was a relatively short ride to midtown Manhattan and the members-only Indulgences Sports Club. As members, they badged themselves in and then went directly to the men's locker room to change clothes while continuing their conversation about market trends.

There were five games already in progress as they entered the massive gym. Geared up, they walked slowly past two of the games watching the energetic play of the various teams until they reached center court where, according to the reader board, their first game was slated to start as soon as the current game ended. They moved up to second place for the series and were looking forward to today's game.

Gregory heard his name called out and the three men looked up into the bleachers. Coming down the steps toward him was Angelique and two attractive security women. No matter where he saw her, she baffled his ability to think straight, thought Gregory.

"Hi," she said, and grinned disarmingly, standing on a step above the floor.

She leaned forward and kissed him, causing a strong current of awareness to streak through him.

"Hi," he said, savoring the taste of her. His libido torqued up another notch.

"These are my friends," she said, and introduced her companions. "Is it all right if we stay to watch your game?"

"Yes, but how did you know I was here?"

"You didn't answer your cellphone, so I called your office to ask what you wanted for dinner. Your assistant said you had left to go to the gym. She wouldn't tell me where, so I called Margo and asked her whether she knew where you were. She told me that you play basketball three times a week. I asked her whether she thought it would be okay to come and watch. She told me where I could find you and she didn't think you'd mind. Is it okay I came?"

"It is, yes," he said, swinging his duffle onto the bleachers and seating her and then himself beside her. The others were enjoying a lively conversation steps away. The Richardson agents were ever vigilant, but always unobtrusive.

"Good because I had to buy a year-long membership for me and my friends to get in here," she said, and laughed. "You didn't mention you still played. I haven't seen you play since you were in college."

"You were very busy with your career during the years I played pro ball."

"I guess I was," she said, distractedly. Looking at him in his scant sportswear was mesmerizing. She looked away trying to come up with something to say to keep from salivating over him when he leaned back with his elbows on the bleacher behind him, legs bent at the knee and wide open. "So, this is a big gym, but I've seen this set-up in Japan. Five games going on simultaneously? Don't you get distracted with so much activity going on beside you?"

"I don't, no. When I'm on the court, my head is in the game." Though he had to admit, at least to himself, having her in attendance was going to cause him to exercise an additional level of control.

"So how does this work?"

"It's a round robin. We're not playing against a clock. We're playing strictly for points. The ten teams play five games; the first five teams to score twenty-one win. Then we slide to the right to set up to play another team on the next court over to the twenty-one count. Then we continue to the next team repeating the process until we've completed five games. Next session we'll play the other teams we don't play today. There are, I believe, sixty teams in the league comprised of former pros and talented amateurs. The teams getting ready to play all work in the financial industries. Moving ahead on the leaders' board depends on how many games each team won and how many points they rack up."

"Both men and women play on the same team?"

"They do, yes.

"A lot of people come to watch you play."

"They're not here to see me play."

Just then two people approached him for a picture and his autograph. He complied and gave Angelique a sardonic smile.

"Well, not *everyone* is here to see me play."

She laughed at his chagrin.

By eleven-thirty his first game was underway. Fortunately for him the game was intense requiring his full focus and concentration. He was in his comfort zone for the first three games. However, the fourth game was a challenge because Alondra was on the opposing team. She took advantage of every opportunity to insinuate herself into his zone, even to the chastisement and consternation of her teammates for being out of position and allowing Gregory's teammates to score and ultimately win the game.

As they walked off the court for a breather, Alondra caught up with Gregory. "I've seen you in the media with your jail bait lately. I thought you were '*just friends*'."

He turned while wiping the perspiration from his face and neck with a towel he took from his duffle. "I told you the truth, Alondra. Angelique is legal and has been a family friend for many years."

"So I've seen in the tabloids, but you never mentioned your sister is Vivian Alexander, the US Olympic Gold Medalist or your brother, Benny Alexander, happened to be an astronaut or your other brother is Kenneth Alexander, former California governor, and head of CompuCorrect Global."

"Our relationship wasn't built on family involvement. As I recall you never mentioned anything at all about your family. We generally talked about business; not personal issues. When you suggested we take our liaison to another level, it was all about the sex. We weren't planning for a home and kids."

"I wasn't open to that direction then."

"Now?"

She moved in closer. "Now I miss what we had."

He backed up a step. "Then our timing is off, Alondra. I'm not open to reinstating a sexual relationship. Friendship, as I said weeks ago, is all I'm prepared to offer."

"If I want more?"

"I've said where I am emotionally and mentally. I won't offer you more."

"I'll take what I can get. How about getting together later tonight for drinks and dinner?"

"That's doable; however, I'll have to bring Angelique along with us."

"I'm not into sharing you with the kid, Greg. Let me know when you find a babysitter so you can spend an evening out with adults. In the interim, be careful you don't get arrested for statutory rape."

That stung, Gregory thought as he watched Alondra saunter away. He still had an uncomfortable feeling about Alondra and her possible motive for wanting to continue a relationship which had absolutely nowhere to go. He didn't claim to be an expert on women and he certainly wasn't egotistical enough to believe he was such a world-class lover. He would have to be more circumspect about what she wanted from him. He had learned a valuable lesson vicariously through his older brothers. One woman almost wrecked Kenneth's life years ago and Benny was, at one point in their early relationship, clueless to Stacy's love for him. Luckily both Kenneth and Benny wised up and now were happily married to the right women. Gregory didn't want to miss any signals which could cause him to lose what was beginning between him and Angelique.

Fortunately the next game had started and he was riding the bench for the first few minutes of play.

Angelique watched the interplay of emotions cross Gregory's and Alondra Martin's faces as they talked. She couldn't hear their conversation, but clearly Alondra wasn't willing to let their relationship fade. It was uncomfortable to watch Gregory watching Alondra's hip-swinging movement as she walked away.

It was one-thirty when Gregory and Jackson Chase were seated in the sports club's restaurant for lunch. Troy had another appointment and couldn't join them.

"So tell me, how are you coming with your plans for your bank?"

"Thanks to you, everything is on track. I had an initial meeting with JRock and JaiHonnah Baylor last week. They're a great team and very intuitive and imaginative. They met me at the two sites in Mitchell County; the proposed bank location and then the tract of land I mentioned on the shores of the Chesapeake Bay. I went ahead and purchased both locations and we worked out a preliminary schedule to begin the construction. I'm using JaiHonnah's uncle's construction company, Lowry Construction. His name is Alroy Lowry and he's located in Bay County, Maryland, not far from my home in Mitchell County. Mr. Lowry has seven adult children, all of whom work in the business with him as subcontractors. I Googled them. They do award-winning work.

"We also kicked around a couple of other ideas I have for construction in the county. If you're interested, I'm open to investments in those other projects. China has already committed. I hadn't had an opportunity to talk with you or anyone else about them."

"I'm always interested in a good investment. Do you have a prospectus prepared?"

"I do, yes. I spent the weekend looking at these other projects because I had such a successful meeting with the Baylors and the Lowrys. I used to follow JRock when he played in the NBA. He mentioned he was a friend of your former brother-in-law, DJ, and your current one, Chuck Montgomery."

"China used to be JRock's comptroller at Baylor Construction for several years before we started CTI. That's how we met. My sister, Vivian, used to be JRock's legal counsel before she became a judge."

"Your sister and JaiHonnah were in undergrad together at Spelman I learned. I also met China's sister, Capri, while I was in DC. China set it up because her sister is an attorney and lobbyist, but I got the distinct impression China had an ulterior motive for putting us together. Apparently China does not care for this guy, Lex Brockington, Capri is dating."

"I didn't know," he said. Nevertheless, he was happy for her. "China never mentioned it."

"Capri and I had dinner. She mentioned you and she used to date. I'm not stepping on hallowed ground, am I?"

Gregory laughed. "No, not at all. Capri and I dated back several years ago, but I was still balling and we couldn't get our schedules synced up too often. I was in New York while she was in DC. I like her as a friend, but that's it. Our separation was mutual and amicable. No hard or residual feelings."

"Good. You've got a rep for dating only one woman at a time. I can't imagine you dating someone and living with Angelique simultaneously."

Their pretend relationship was making the rounds on the rumor mill just as they planned, but it was only a half-truth. They were living together under the same roof, but not in the same bed as most people assumed.

"So you're still dating Yvonne Kincaid and planning to start something with Capri McAlister?"

"No, not at all. My relationship with Yvonne has about run its course. I'm not open to a more-involved relationship with her, particularly if and when I plan to move back to Maryland.

"As for Capri McAlister, she's an interesting woman, and, if it were not for the professional relationship I'm exploring with her, I might have been interested. As you probably know, she generally works Capitol Hill and the international arena, but she's also worked the Maryland State House and legislature. The political landscape is in her wheelhouse. She agreed to take me on as a client to get my bank chartered through the Maryland power structure. I can handle things at the county level."

"If anyone can do it, it would be Capri. As I recall, she also has international clients."

"She does, yes. It's going to be worth it to get re-established in my home town."

"I know what you mean. My great-grandaunt offered an opportunity to me to move back to South Carolina and I plan to take her up on her offer. I'm thinking of doing what you're doing."

"Starting a state bank?"

"Yes. Like your Mitchell County, Summer County is fairly rural so there aren't a lot of banks in the community or in the state *per se*. It has the largest land mass in the state, but it has among the smallest populations. Based on the last few Census reports, young people are moving out of Summer County to attend college and start careers elsewhere. How ya gonna keep 'em down on the farm after they've seen gay Parie," he joked. "I'm doing some research to determine whether a state-chartered bank headquartered in Atlantic Beach or along the Grand Strand would be viable. Justin McCoy, head of McCoy Industries, is a South Carolinian and believes a new bank would be welcomed in South Carolina."

"I think he's right. North Carolina is the big banking state around Charlotte, but not South Carolina. I believe you'd do well there. Isn't your father a senator to the South Carolina legislature?"

"He is, yes, and I've discussed this with him when he was in town recently, but he can't participate with any proposal I may submit before the state to charter a bank. However, I do have other connections I can use to lobby for a favorable vote for state-chartered banks and maybe even a regional bank in time."

"What about Angelique? What would happen to your relationship if you moved?"

"I haven't discussed this with her yet."

"Good luck with that. Although I'm looking forward to returning to Mitchell County, it's going to be difficult being there where the woman I love is married to someone else."

That made Gregory wonder how he would feel if Angelique married someone else and she and his sister were still as tight as they are now. He didn't like the feeling that possibility brought to his gut.

"Her name is Jackie, by the way. Jacqueline Alicia Conner. She's married to Robert Mitchell of the Maryland Mitchells. Their history is prevalent in Maryland from the time of slavery."

"Does she know how you feel about her?"

"No, she doesn't. I did something really stupid back in high school she didn't deserve. She stopped speaking to me."

"That long ago?"

Jackson laughed self-deprecatingly. "Yeah, yeah, so it wasn't *that* long ago, but at seventeen, it was monumental."

"Yeah, how well I remember," said Gregory.

"I spoke with Peter today. He's on his way home to marry Joyce, but you can't mention anything to her."

"That's great news," Angelique said, over Beef Bourguignon, Red Cabbage and cranberries, and Fettuccine. There was an apple pudding cooling on the kitchen counter, but her words lacked enthusiasm.

Gregory was thoroughly enjoying the meal, but put down his fork and gave Angelique his undivided attention. "Is something wrong?"

She shrugged then put down her fork and rested her chin on her palm, her elbow on the table. "You've dated a lot of women, haven't you?"

Talk about a question coming out of left field. "Uh, yeah? I'm a guy. I'm not gay or bisexual. I date women exclusively."

"You used to date my cousin, Carmen. Why didn't that work out?"

"We were in college at the time. We graduated. She went to medical school in California; I went into the NBA in New York. She met and married someone she fell in love with. As you know she's happily married and practicing medicine in Peru."

"Were you in love with her?"

"I haven't been *in love* with anyone. Why all the questions?"

"I saw you talking with Alondra today at the gym. She seemed pretty intense."

"Ah," he breathed as understanding came. "Is that why you left without saying goodbye?"

"No, well, maybe yes."

He leaned forward, his arms folded and braced on the table; his muscles bulged standing out in stark relief. "Alondra asked me out tonight. I agreed, but only on the condition you join us." He palmed her chin and kissed her mouth. "She didn't care for those terms."

Her eyes sparkled and her mouth bowed into a beatific smile.

"Yes, I date, Angelique, but only one woman at a time. Anyone who knows me and even the tabloids know it to be my usual MO. Right now, Angel Face, everyone believes we're dating. That's what we're supposed to let people believe."

"So it's just for show? Our dating I mean?"

"There's no one here, but us and I just kissed you. I usually kiss the women I date."

Her smile was again luminous. Whereas she had been picking at her food, she began to eat again this time with gusto. Greg followed suit and even had a second helping. She was an excellent chef.

Later that evening, Gregory loaded the dishwasher and cleaned the kitchen. He brewed a cup of coffee to drink with the generous portion of apple pudding he dished up to eat while he watched a movie.

Angelique had gone up stairs to call the designer Carlos Ortega to talk with him about a special wedding dress for Joyce and a honeymoon wardrobe for her trip to Australia. Joyce was not a petite woman and usually had difficulty choosing flattering clothes for herself. Carlos had a line of women's apparel for full-figured ladies. Joyce struggled to keep her weight down and was successful, but her bone structure was heavy. After all, she had one brother, Chuck, who was big boned and just an inch shy of seven feet tall. She had a sedimentary career, but of late she had installed a stationary bike in her office. She would get on it and ride several times each day. Angelique had an idea of the perfect wedding dress for her. She discussed it with Margo and Aretha because they also would be Joyce's bridesmaids. They agreed to make the trousseau a gift from all of them. That task completed, she decided to join Gregory to watch a movie.

He was comfortably stretched out on a wide divan when Angelique joined him.

"Is this Miguel's latest movie release?"

"It is, yes. I haven't made time to watch it before now."

"I haven't either," she said, as she snuggled in under his right arm and laid her head on his shoulder. Her right hand palmed the center of his T-shirt-covered chest over his heart. They silently watched the movie. At some point, Angelique had snaked her right hand under his T-shirt and was playing with his left raisin-like nipple. He was as hard as epee, but he didn't stop her ministration. Her soft, even breaths told him she was asleep. He kissed the top of her head, covered them both with a chair blanket and watched the movie to its conclusion. With a flick of the remote, he turned off the television, dimmed the lights, and slipped into a comfortable sleep with Angelique in his arms.

Angelique woke nestled snugly in Gregory's warm embrace. She could see the sky beginning to brighten outside the picture windows. She liked the feel of waking in Gregory arms in the spacious silence. Her right knee was wedged between his thighs and her right hand splayed across his heart and warm skin. She tilted up her head to look her fill of his handsome features. His slight beard and mustache gave him an even sexier appearance. His dark brown, wavy hair was neatly trimmed and his eyebrows were a perfect complement to his countenance. He had a strong jaw, a clever mouth which did wonderful things to her, and brows and lashes that would make most women envious. There was nothing about Gregory that didn't thrill her.

She lightly ran her finger tips across his mouth. He puckered his lips and kissed each one and then her palm. Slowly, to her delight, he opened his eyes and searched hers.

"Did you sleep well?" he asked, while stretching and yawning.

She nodded and crawled on top of his nearly prone body facing him. Palming his hands she locked her fingers with his, stretching his arms above his head. The thick muscles in his shoulders stood out in proud relief. Slowly by degrees, with her eyes open on his, she leaned forward and kissed him. He watched her as intently as she watched him throughout the joining of their mouths. The evidence of his desire for her pressed strongly at the apex of her wide-opened thighs.

"Greg," she breathed his name, "please . . ."

"No," he said, his eyes still intent on hers. He brought her hands to his lips, kissed them before lifting her from his lap as if she weighed nothing and setting her on her feet.

Frustrated, she stood and watched him walk away from her.

Gregory was so hard he could have broken bricks. He wanted her in his bed, but he knew they weren't ready for that irrevocable step. She was a virgin, a precious gift she should save for the man she would marry. It wasn't a gift he would take carelessly if there wasn't going to be permanency in a relationship. Still, he didn't know where their feelings would take them and if it all ended after a short whirlwind romance, he had to face his family and hers. He wouldn't risk her reputation on a relationship which was only a month old.

He turned his face up to the shower above his head and turned the body sprays on full force to beat his sensitive nerve ending into submission. He had to get out of there and go to his office or he would have Angelique spread eagle on her back and be deep inside her.

The high-pitched scream alerted Gregory that Peter Calloway had finally put in an appearance. People in the office came on the run to see what all the commotion was about.

Hands in his pockets, Gregory ambled out of his office, leaned against his door jamb, and watched while Joyce, securely wrapped in Peter's arms, ravished his face with kisses.

Applause began to ripple around the executive offices leading to hoots, whistles, and cat calls. Finally, the ardent lovers, with faces wreathed in smiles, realized they had a relatively large audience. Joyce unlatched her legs from around Peter's waist and climbed down his tall, but still football-toned body. She clung to him and buried her face in his chest, tears flowing down her flushed features.

"Hey, get a room," Gregory called out as he walked toward his former college housemate. He found himself sandwiched between his friends in a group hug.

"You're the best damn friend—!"

"Yeah, yeah, so you've said. How was your flight?"

"Man!" he said, expressively. "It was awesome. That Irish band was off the charts and the charter flight had everything from soup to nuts! I was treated like royalty."

"You knew he was coming and didn't tell me?" Joyce accused.

"And spoil his surprise? Not on a bet," said Gregory.

"Babe, if it wasn't for him, I'd still be in Australia trying to get on a flight on standby status going half way around the world in the opposite direction."

"Well, I guess it's okay you kept it from me this time, but don't do it again," she fussed without heat.

"Why don't you two get out of here? It's the week before Thanksgiving. Not a lot is going to be happening during the US holiday."

"Joyce?" Peter asked, warming to the idea of getting her alone.

She smiled up at him. "Let me get my coat and purse," she said, and walked back to her office.

"That's my girl," Peter said, quietly. "I missed her like crazy. Thanks, man, for giving me the heads-up I could have lost her."

"She's in love with you, Peter, but ten years is a long time to wait."

"I realize it now. She's just always been there for me supporting my dreams. Without her, it would have meant nothing. I hope someday you'll feel this way about someone."

"Maybe I will," said Gregory as he watched the unadulterated joy on Joyce's and Peter's faces.

Hugging each other, they headed to the elevator.

Gregory went back to work and tried really hard not to think of Angelique. Ultimately, he failed, packed it in for the day, and went home early. He could also get a jump on the upcoming holiday season. With Angelique along, his family would definitely read her attendance with him as a statement of his intentions. He wondered whether it was.

Chapter 13

"Oh look at the beautiful baby!" exclaimed Angelique as she and Gregory entered the front parlor of The Summer House, a huge bed and breakfast in Summer County, South Carolina. The place was an old, refurbished antebellum mansion, owned by his first cousin Satarah James Johnson and her second husband, Summer County Fire Chief Douglas Johnson. Angelique, Gregory, Aretha, and the Joyner brothers were arriving early to see what they could do to help with the preparations for Thanksgiving dinner. Angelique reached for Douglas' and Satarah's newborn, Katherine Lynn Johnson. Satarah, once a Registered Nurse, gave up her fulltime medical career as the head Emergency Room administrative nurse to become a stay-at-home mom and manage The Summer House fulltime. She and her family lived on the one-hundred-acre grounds, an inheritance passed down to her from her maternal side of the family. As an excellent cook, she handled the breakfast meals for the business while raising four young, teenaged boys and now two baby girls under two-years-old with her husband of only three years.

Satarah's eldest boy, Benson Whitfield Johnson, she had with Jonathan Jeffrey Whitfield "JoJeff" when she was barely fifteen. Once he found out about her pregnancy, he ran off and joined the Army or in actuality was scared off by her father and the county sheriff who threatened to have him arrested for statutory rape if he didn't leave the area.

Three years later, JoJeff returned when Satarah was of legal age and married her, but by then her father, Obadiah Baker James, a local jackleg preacher, had sent her away and tricked her into giving up their baby for adoption. Not satisfied with being a husband to her, JoJeff fathered twins, Johnathan and Jeffrey Whitfield, with Satarah's older sister, Carlotta

James. JoJeff and Carlotta had carried on an affair under Satarah's nose and then for a second time he ran off, this time with her older sister leaving Satarah to raise their boys alone while she continued to search for the son she had given away. Carlotta had not returned home to Summer County, but JoJeff was back after ten years and, seeing how prosperous his former wife had become, was attempting to insinuate himself into Satarah's life again. Years later the son she was tricked into giving up was found in a Chicago orphanage and returned to her by her soon-to-be husband, Douglas Johnson.

Then there was Donovan Johnson, a boy who Douglas and his former, now deceased, first wife adopted.

She never denied JoJeff the right to see the three sons he fathered; one with her and two with her sister, but his arrival, as her family assembled for Thanksgiving dinner, was unwelcomed.

"*Whoa!* Who is this pretty woman?" exclaimed JoJeff.

Angelique heard the man, but she didn't recognize him as one of the Alexander family members and her attention was on the baby in her arms. "Aren't you just the sweetest angel?" Angelique crooned to the bright-eyed baby who gurgled and grinned showing bare, pink gums.

"She's the super model, Angel, dad," fourteen-year-old Benson supplied, eager to gain his father's time and attention. When he was rescued in Chicago and brought back to meet his biological mother, he was also curious about his father. He asked his cousin, Donald Dixon, to help him find his father. Reluctantly, but with Satarah's and Douglas' permission, Donald found JoJeff in Las Vegas within days and returned him to Summer County. Benson had been desperate to forge a relationship with his biological father ever since. "She lives in New York and that's her brother over there talking with Whitney Ivy and Linda. He's the actor, Miguel Menendez. He's in the action movie **Tight Wire** showing in the theatres now."

"You don't say," crooned JoJeff watching Angelique with a critical eye.

"Why are you still here, JoJeff?" questioned Satarah, his former wife, as she came into the front parlor from seeing to the preparations in the kitchen and smaller dining room.

"I thought we'd stay here, my boys and me, and have dinner with the family," he said, grinning and attempting to pull her into an embrace without success.

"Not today. If the boys want to go to your house or to your parents' house for Thanksgiving dinner, then it's their decision." She absently ran her hands over Benson's shoulders. After losing him for nearly fifteen years, she took every opportunity to touch her first-born no matter how casual the contact.

"Oh, don't be so hard on your husband, baby. You know you want me here."

"*Former* husband, JoJeff, a fact you seem to want to forget."

"How do I know we're really divorced? I never signed any papers, SaraJo."

"Ask Judge Malcolm Galloway, if you're not clear. He granted my petition for divorce after you and my sister deserted me taking every red cent we had," she said, without heat. "Or, I saw my cousin, Vivian, a moment ago in the Rose Parlor. Why don't you go ask her about it? I'm sure she can probably call up a copy of the divorce decree on her laptop and print out a copy for you in my office."

His frown was petulant. "That woman never liked me," he mumbled aggrieved. "She's probably the one who talked you into giving up on our marriage."

"Regardless, JoJeff, she's legally Mrs. Douglas Johnson now," Doug said, as he entered the parlor carrying his and Satarah's two-year-old daughter, Arianna Mariah Johnson. He leaned forward and kissed Satarah's waiting mouth.

Gregory observed the exchange between his cousin, Satarah Josephine, and her former husband, JoJeff, but wasn't sure of the dynamics. He liked and respected her new husband, the Fire Chief, Douglas Johnson, and moved toward him.

"G, how are you, man?" Douglas happily asked, giving Gregory a one-arm, brotherly hug.

"I'm doing well, Chief, and how are you, Ari?" he said, accepting the pretty little two-year-old when she reached for him.

"Up! Go up!" Arianna pleaded.

Gregory knew what it meant and he tossed her in the air while she giggled and squealed her delight, and then clung to his neck giving him a sloppy, noisy kiss on the mouth.

"Are you enjoying your new career?" Douglas asked.

"I am, yes. I particularly like how it allows me to attend more family gatherings like this one. So, how are things with you?" They continued catching up with each other's lives.

JoJeff was essentially a non-entity as conversation continued among Satarah's family members who were gathering for dinner.

"Hey, dad?" Jonathan, Jr., hailed, coming into the parlor followed by his twin, Jeffrey, and Dejon and Keaton. "Would you come help us put up the volleyball net?"

It did not escape anyone's notice the twin boys went to Douglas for help and essentially ignored the presence of their biological father, JoJeff, in the same room. However, JoJeff was attempting to chat up Angelique and turning on the heavy charm to win her awareness of his presence. Benson was at his elbow, still attempting to insinuate himself into his father's conversation to gain his attention.

"Are you okay with Ari?" asked Douglas.

"Sure, go ahead and help the children," said Gregory. "I'll keep this pretty lady company."

"Thanks," said Douglas, "and, by the way, you might want to rescue Angelique."

Gregory looked over his shoulder and noticed Angelique was still crooning to the new baby. Just then, she looked up, and ignoring JoJeff, smiled at him. She excused herself and moved toward Gregory still carrying Katherine Lynn.

"Isn't she a doll, Greg?" Angelique asked, positioning Katherine so he could see her.

"Sista," Ari exclaimed, clapping her hands and grinning.

"She is, yes," said Gregory, but when Angelique looked up at him, he was momentarily taken by the effervescence of her radiant smile.

"Did you notice how big her sister, Arianna, has grown?" he asked while tickling Ari's tummy and making the little girl squeal, giggling, then burying herself further into Gregory's embrace.

"Hi, Uncle Greg, Angelique," said Whitney Ivy, his brother, Benjamin's tall, fourteen-year-old-daughter, giving both kisses and warm hugs. "Ooooh is this Katherine Lynn?" she asked, positioning herself so she could see the baby. "Oooh, she's so pretty!"

"Let me see," said Linda, Vivian's and Chuck's oldest daughter. Whitney and Linda were cousins and the best of friends. Linda is a prima ballerina now in her teens recently back from a European tour. No one thought about the fact Linda lost her biological father in the Iraqi War, her mother and younger brother in a car accident. She spent years under Derrick Jackson's medical care in an orphanage until Vivian and Derrick legally adopted her. Now she was simply viewed as a precious member of the family.

"Hey, Uncle Greg, have you seen Jonathan and Jeffrey?"

"Hey, Bryan. Yes, I saw them. They went outside with their father to set up the volleyball net."

"Cool!" said Bryan, another of Vivian's and Chuck's adopted children. He kissed and hugged Angelique before he kissed both Arianna and Katherine and then scurried away. To look at him one would not know he was born with deformed lungs. In fact, none of Chuck's and Vivian's adopted multicultural, rainbow coalition children looked anything but in the best of health.

"Oh, let us get our hands on these babies," said Bernard, Gregory's father and Romello Dixon, his uncle, as they gathered the girls into their arms.

Angelique looked decidedly reluctant to relinquish the newborn, Gregory noticed. He put his arm around her waist and she laid her head on his shoulder.

"I want to have a baby," she whispered, still looking at the little girls as Bernard and Romello moved to seating near an open window. Then she looked up at him. "I want to have a baby with you, Greg." She put up a hand to forestall any comment he might make. "If it can't happen for whatever reason; if you won't give me a baby, then I'll be artificially inseminated. It's your choice. I'm going to see if I can help Satarah in the kitchen," she said, and then walked away.

He stood dumbfounded and watched her go. He noted JoJeff also tracked her movements and then slipped out of the parlor behind her.

"Hey, little brother," Benny said, finding Gregory standing looking wise and otherwise. "Something wrong?"

"No, not really."

Benny had trained too many young airmen and women not to be able to recognize trouble brewing in his younger brother's demeanor. He was a US Air Force jet fighter pilot, astronaut, and now a General, a member of the Joint Chief's staff of advisors, stationed in Japan. His responsibilities included the Air Forces' segment of the US Pacific Command coordinating the RIMPAC exercises. More importantly, he was a father. He knew when to step in. "Let's walk, G," he said to Gregory and went out a pair of French doors onto a covered, open-air, deep, wrap-around veranda.

The young cousins were playing spirited games of volleyball, tennis, basketball, badminton and croquet in different segments of the yard so Benny and Gregory sauntered in the opposite direction. Other family members were arriving and unloading copious amounts of food and drink. There would be over a hundred people in attendance. Bernard Alexander, Benny's and Gregory's father, was the fifth in a line of thirteen siblings. Only his older, late sister, Beatrice, and her husband, Rick, who both died in a car crash in California, would not be there, but their nine children would be in attendance with their spouses and children. Siblings, first-second-and-third generation cousins, their spouses and offspring were a close-knit group who were never out of touch with each other. At last count, there were more than thirty first cousins, more than sixty second cousins, *ad infinitum*. Including spouses, the Alexander clan alone was legion.

"Is this a private party or can anyone join?" Kenneth asked, coming abreast of his younger brothers, Benjamin and Gregory.

"Just giving young blood time to tell me what's up with him," said Benny.

"Probably something to do with Angelique," offered Kenneth.

"Ah," Benny intoned, understanding dawning, "that's understandable. Are you ready to go to the knee and then make an announcement?"

Gregory shrugged. "Until a few weeks ago, I was sleeping with Alondra Martin," he said, candidly.

"The Gold Medalist?" asked Benny.

"The same."

"I thought you were seeing the sommelier, Merissa Talbert."

"Off and on."

"You have feelings for Alondra Martin?"

"Heat, not even lust."

"Anyone else?"

"Capri McAllister, China McAllister's sister. Capri is an attorney, a lobbyist who is a partner in her law firm, Kit, Kenmore and McAllister, and lives in DC. That was a while ago when I was still pounding the hardwood. We couldn't get the logistics right often enough to suit either of us."

"So this thing for you with Angelique is new?"

"More a renewal of something I've felt for some time; years in fact. It's more intense now, bordering on lust probably because she's living under my roof."

The brows on Benny's handsome face winged up. "Living together? That's not like you at all. I haven't been closely involved, but from what Stacy tells me, which isn't much, someone has been spying on Angelique?" Benny said, referring to his wife, Navy Admiral Stacy Greene Alexander, an intelligence operative and also an advisor to the Joint Chiefs of Staff. The extent of her knowledge a mystery to him. They had seven children together; two sets of triplets, girls and boys and their eldest daughter Whitney Ivy. His wife was a fiercely protective mother who loved him and their children with a passion.

"That and the financial fix she's in," added Kenneth, who watched Gregory with a warm and steady stare.

Gregory felt Kenneth's eyes on him as the three of them settled in a wide, round, screened gazebo Kenneth and Douglas Johnson built years earlier. He looked up to meet his eldest brother's eyes. He wouldn't treat Kenneth's concern with his usual blasé, matter-of-factness. The weighty silence continued while the three brothers stood with feet apart, heads up, and hands in pockets. Vivian and Aretha joined their brothers and the stalemate ended.

"He doesn't know the answers yet," said Vivian, attuned to the nature of the conversation as if she had been a party to the discussion about her younger brother from the beginning.

"She's my BFF, but it should not determine the direction you take with her, Gregory," added Aretha. "If it don't fit, don't force it." She was just as perceptive as was Vivian and attuned to his concerns. She was considered the family oracle.

It warmed Gregory's heart his brothers and sisters understood him so completely and had always supported the person he is. "I believe I'll know when it's right."

"You will," said Kenneth. "We trust you and your judgment."

"If she's the right fit for you, she will be welcomed into the family," said Benny.

Spontaneously, they momentarily formed a tight circle with arms around each other. Then they dispersed to greet arriving family members and help with the final preparations for dinner.

While the five Alexander siblings were outside, Angelique and her mother, Anna, joined Satarah, Sylvia Benson Alexander, Olivia Alexander Dixon, the Mayor of Goodwill, and other family members in the industrial-sized kitchen putting the finishing touches on the food.

"That's beautiful," said Satarah as she watched Angelique enhance the dishes with garnishes. She sprinkled parsley flakes on the long pan of creamy potatoes *au gratin* giving it a festive appearance.

"Thanks, Satarah. What do you think, *Momi*?"

"Yes, yes, I like very much. I think pimentos for the green beans, yes?" Anna said, her Peruvian accent still a whisper in her warm, soft voice.

"Yes," agreed Satarah who went into her walk-in pantry to find a few jars.

Seeing his opportunity, JoJeff followed her in, closing the door behind him.

Jars in hand, Satarah turned abruptly to look at him. *"Seriously?"* Sarcasm coated the word and the expression on her face.

"You know you want me, Sara Jo," he said, grinning. "You're only with the muscle man to make me jealous."

"It's always about you, isn't it? It's about what you want regardless of what others need. Well, it's true I loved you once, JoJeff, but it was long ago when I was still a child. We share a son, Benson, who wants to get to know you, but it was the 'muscle man,' my husband, who went out of his way to find Benson for me, the son I was forced to give away years ago when you deserted me the first time. He found *your* son and brought him home to me. Why? Because that's the type of man he is. Three of my boys don't share my husband's blood, but he'd give his life for any one of them, and for the boy he adopted. Do you actually think I'd want you, a man who took my sister to our bed behind my back and had babies with her while we were still married and then ran off with her leaving me with your babies, over a man like Douglas Johnson? Really? You're delusional if you do," her spine stiffening ramrod straight. It was clear she held JoJeff beneath her contempt. "You're just someone I used to know, but if you keep easing up on Angelique, my cousin, Gregory Clayton, will give you a beat down the likes of which you've never seen. I'll hold his coat for him while he does it. How do you like me now?"

She brushed past him, back into the kitchen.

The applause was thunderous for Aretha Grace Alexander and Fenster Jones as they completed playing a medley of classical music on the piano and violin, respectively, accompanied by an array of other family members. After dinner, the Alexander clan was comfortably assembled in The Summer House's main ballroom enjoying the performances of talented family members.

Next up were Whitney Ivy Alexander and Miguel Menendez-Gaza who began playing a number of classical guitar medleys and then, fifteen minutes into their show, broke out in a jazzy Latin rhythm and had people rocking in their seats or dancing in the aisles around the perimeter of the ballroom.

Whitney's triplet sisters, five years younger than her, joined her and Miguel to serenade the family with their soon-to-be-released CD, the sixth in their catalog. The blended voices intermingled with the guitar riffs from Miguel and Whitney caused a hush to fall on the room. Not even a baby cried, though there were many in the ballroom.

Angelique managed to get her hands on a peacefully sleeping Katherine Lynn, again, humming along and swaying rhythmically to the Latin style music her brother and Gregory's niece produced. Gregory sat next to her holding Arianna, her back to his chest.

The family musicians played for a performance by Linda as she danced a segment of the opera *Firebird*.

Gregory was enormously proud of his family and with good reason. They were all people he not only loved, but also genuinely liked and would want to befriend even if they were not related by blood or marriage. He looked around the ballroom at the interracial nature of many of his families' spouses and offspring. All, from the youngest to the oldest, wore a gold chain around their necks that read FAMILY. In the ballroom they had their own Rainbow Coalition. Yet the family blended into a strong unit, like the never-ending chains they sported. They had people from diverse backgrounds and heritages represented, everyone contributing to the family collective. They had so much to be thankful for on this holiday. As he watched Angelique cuddling Katherine Lynn and heard her humming quietly along with his niece and her brother, she grew another dimension in his affection.

The ballroom dance floor was crowded after the performances ended, but the little ones were dropping off as the night grew later. Parents were putting the babies to bed in The Summer House's many bedrooms while they continued to enjoy the Thanksgiving holiday festivities. These were the times he missed when he was away following his basketball career.

A hot and cold buffet was set up in one of the smaller dining rooms to serve the remaining food and for the breakfast buffet Satarah, Anna, and Angelique added to the menu as the clock neared midnight.

It was a good thing, Gregory thought, he could dance off the pounds he must have consumed that day. He had played an energetic game of basketball with his brothers, cousins and brother-in-law, Chuck, on their team, but he and Douglas lost at tennis against Satarah and Angelique. He would not soon live down the defeat.

Now, as he swayed to the sounds of his Aunt Mariah's soulful singing with Angelique in his arms, he let the good feelings of the day settle in around him. These were the special times he missed while he was away during the eight years he steadfastly followed his career. With the scent of Angelique's hair stirring his senses, he let his eyes close.

"What time are you leaving in the morning?"

"Wheels up at five."

"This will be the first time we won't be sleeping under the same roof since I came and took up residence in your home. I'm going to miss you."

"I'll be away only until Sunday. In the meantime you'll be able to spend some quality time with your mother and the females in my family. You should be fine and safe without me for a few days."

"I know. Internet shopping. It kind of takes the fun out of bargain hunting in the crowded stores in New York City after Thanksgiving. However, we're going to the outlet shops near Atlantic Beach. Is there something special you want me to buy for your family or the boys?"

"I've got my family covered. For Dejon and Keaton, clothes and shoes are always in demand. They keep growing out of everything and it's difficult for Mrs. Joyner to keep up. You probably know some designers who specialize in clothes to fit the boys."

"I do, yes. In fact this buyer from McCoy's Department Store has been tracking me down about being a judge for a pre-Christmas fashion show for teens. Maybe I'll be able to convince her to let Dejon model some of the clothes. Usually young models get to keep the clothes they model. It's great advertising for a designer's line in this demographic group. Even though he's not yet a teen, maybe even Keaton could do it too. They are tall, slim, handsome boys."

Gregory chuckled. "I think they'd both get a kick out of doing something like that."

"It's how Miguel and I got started in the business, thanks to Bill. He told me he tried to get you to model, but you refused."

"He did try and I did a few fashion shows with my NBA teammates for charity functions. We helped raise a lot of money especially after the Olympic successes."

"I know. I have pictures," she said, giggling.

"You actually kept pictures of me?"

"Every one I could get my hands on, yes. Especially the ones I found on Aretha's family blog."

"I have to admit I also have pictures of your magazine covers."

She looked up into his eyes, smiling as they continued to dance. She put her arms up around his neck. "I like knowing you did it. That you kept pictures of me. It means you were thinking of me."

He tucked her head back under his chin and brought her body flush against his. He realized she had always been in his thoughts without knowing what the revelation had actually meant. His infatuation with her started when he first met her when she was a pre-teen; not more than a little girl in pigtails. He was already in his teenage years when they met the first summer after she and her family came to live in the townhouse in Georgetown. She was recuperating from a serious case of Rheumatic Fever. He would come to DC during the summer to stay with Vivian and work earning pocket money while he was still in high school. Benny arranged for him to work a summer job at the Pentagon helping employees solve IT problems with computer programs. He was a competent computer geek able to read and write computer code. It was interesting work, but not something he wanted to make into a career the way Kenneth had, nor was he interested in serving in the military the way Benny did. Mostly, being in the DC metropolitan area during the summer allowed him to visit a lot of college campuses in several states to determine where he wanted to spend his collegiate career. Though he had offers to attend a full array of colleges and universities on either an academic or athletic scholarship, the University of Virginia ranked highest on his list. He never regretted making the decision to attend for his undergrad and graduate degrees. Now he realized it also kept him in close proximity to Washington, DC, and Angelique.

When the music changed from his aunt singing to a recording of the line dance, Footloose, he excused himself and made his way to the buffet to get a helping of Apple Brown Betty before it was all gone. His mother came out of the kitchen into the buffet room carrying a fresh tray of the piping hot dessert.

"Here, let me help you with that," he said, taking the large, oblong, metal pan by the handles while she removed the other nearly empty pan from the hot buffet.

"Thank you, sweetheart," Sylvia said, as her son placed the new tray in the empty space where the other one had been.

"Don't take the tray away. It has just enough Apple Brown Betty to fill the hole in my stomach," he joked. He scooped up the great-smelling treat into a bowl while his mother looked on shaking her head. He topped it with a generous helping of Vanilla Bean ice cream

"I don't know how you manage to stay so trim considering the amount of food you manage to consume."

"High metabolism and great genes, thanks to you and dad," he managed while polishing off the last bite. Then he coaxed his mother into dancing with him. She followed his lead easily enough. She was a great dancer and she and his father enjoyed dancing together at the Friday night fish fry in Goodwill's Town Hall. Sometimes his parents would spend the weekend in Columbia, the South Carolina state capitol, where Bernard was an elected senator from his district or in Charleston at a hotel just to be alone together on the ocean-front. They were married for over forty years and were so blatantly in love they still glowed with happiness. That was the kind of love Gregory wanted for himself. To look back on a lifetime with a wife he was still so passionately in love with.

"I saw you dancing with Angelique earlier. You two look good together."

"Mom, if you're working on suggesting it's time for me to settle down..."

"*Psshaw*, baby boy. I trust you to know when you're ready for that step and to make a good decision about who to spend the rest of your life with. You don't need my intrusion into your decision-making process."

"Thanks, mom," he said, and kissed her temple as they continued to dance.

"On the other hand," she said, laughing when he sighed dramatically, "I am concerned about Angelique's level of maturity. She's a sweet, wonderful girl who I'd welcome into the family as your wife should she be the one you want."

"But?"

"No, buts necessarily. It's just she may need to mature a little more to be a good partner for you."

"Why, what do you see, mom?"

"Angelique, and to a certain extent, Miguel, too, have been sheltered since they came to the America from Peru. Private schools were great for the academics, but they haven't had a lot of life experiences."

"Whatever doesn't kill you makes you stronger."

"Exactly. Angelique went to Wellesley, a fine college, for a hot two years before she quit to go to Le Cordon Bleu in France. She finished the program, but rather than honing her craft as an employee working in the restaurant industry, she embarked on starting her own restaurant in one of the toughest markets in the world. I admire her need to be an entrepreneur, but at only twenty, I question the wisdom of her decision. She's creative and her restaurant is unique, but she started the business without any background in management. Hence the dilemma you found her in. Just because you can *afford* to do a thing doesn't always follow you *should* do it. Nevertheless, I predict, with your guidance, she will do very well."

"You're right, mom. Some of her decisions have not been the best in the short or long run. I think she's still trying to find her niche. She attained extraordinary notoriety as a super model and actress, but again what to do was dictated by people who gathered around her."

"Don't misunderstand my meaning. She's extremely talented, however, whether she's found her way on her own two feet has yet to be determined.

"You're a young man who set goals for yourself and moved step by step to achieve whatever you set out to do. Your father and I admire that trait in you. You're your own man because of it. When you accomplished each task, you set new, tougher goals for yourself. You've been independent making most of your own decisions since you were in puberty. Your father and I had only to stand by and watch."

"I didn't have a choice with Aretha around cracking the whip."

Sylvia chuckled. "Yes, you're right, but your sister did it because she is so enormously proud of you. She loves all of her siblings, but especially you because you always included her in everything you did. Your father and I never had to worry about where Aretha was or what she was doing. For you she wasn't the pesky baby sister; she was your best friend."

"She still is and the fact she's Angelique's best friend makes an intimate relationship with Angelique much more of a risk for all of us."

"I know the fact she's still a virgin would weigh heavily on your mind."

"She told you?"

"We talked during the time we spent at your home in New York. She's at a crossroads in her life. You know she has been infatuated with you since she was an adolescent and now you've become her super hero because you're seeing her through a difficult period.

"Don't worry so much about being on the right path, son, because you are. I've known you since nine months before you drew your first breath of air. You have always been in the right place in your thinking at the right time. There's no need to feel apprehensive about what you should or should not do. You'll do the right thing for both you and her because you don't know how to do anything else. You always do. Even though you may not be able to change certain situations, like her age and level of maturity, you can at least change your reaction to them."

"Grant me the serenity to accept the things that I can't change, the strength and knowledge to change the things that I can, and the wisdom to know the difference."

"Exactly," Sylvia said, as the music ended. She rose on her toes and kissed his cheek.

He hugged her tightly. She and his father were always solid role models and a source of strength and guidance for him and his siblings. They spoke the wisdom of their ancestry.

Chapter 14

The Adventurer Executive Airline jet set down just after dawn at the Eagle County, Colorado, airport, just thirty minutes from the ski resort in Vale. It carried a contingent of Alexander family males and their children for their traditional, post-Thanksgiving Day, ski trip. In previous years Gregory was unable to attend because of his professional basketball schedule and certain contractual limitations. This was the first year since the tradition started he could attend. He had Dejon and Keaton in tow. They spent the previous week on his families' farms and had not fully recovered from his family's large, rambunctious gatherings. Now they had three days of skiing ahead of them; something else these city boys had never experienced, but Gregory was confident his young nieces, nephews, and cousins would have the boys on the slopes in no time.

They deplaned and boarded Adventurer's ground transportation buses which would take them to the Adventurer Ski Resort where Vivian's former husband's chalet was located on a ten-acre rise at the base of the North Slope. After her first husband's death, Vivian had the large home remodeled so the men in her family could share the two-level, six-thousand-square-foot, eight bedroom, eight-and-a-half-bath home while the children slept in sleeping bags on cots in the great room. With fifty children, teens, and ten adult males they would be bursting at the seams. Their meals would be catered for the three days or they would eat out at one of the many restaurants between ski runs.

Wives and female significant others were not a part of the getaway, but were given the task of doing the Christmas shopping. Gregory left Angelique in the care of her mother and his female family members.

They were on their way to the McCoy's Oceans Inn Spa and Resort near Myrtle Beach, South Carolina.

The chalet was huge, but warm and inviting when the buses arrived to unload their passengers. When Dejon and Keaton stood in the falling snow, their mouths dropped open at seeing the gigantic, pristine and picturesque snow-covered mountains surrounding them. Fenster, Miguel, and Gregory were no less impressed.

"Come on," James Dixon called out. "Those slopes are calling my name."

"Let's get settled in, eat, and hit the slopes," Kenneth encouraged.

They put their duffels away in locker room-like cubbies and descended on the breakfast buffet awaiting their arrival. Scrambled eggs, hot biscuits, hash browns, sausage, kippers, and bacon, fresh fruit, coffee, hot cocoa, and fresh-squeezed juices fed the hoard before they donned heavy outerwear sufficient for the cold, snowy weather.

At the ski lodge store, Gregory, Fenster, Miguel, Dejon, and Keaton were outfitted with goggles, skis, and poles in preparation for their first lessons while the rest of the young, experienced family members headed out with their adult chaperones for the many ski lifts arranged according to their skill levels.

Later that day, by the time Gregory and his crew of beginners assembled for dinner at an all-you-can-eat buffet with the rest of his family, his calves and thigh muscles were burning. He was a well-toned athlete, but skiing demanded another level of skill to navigate on the snow. Fenster, a concert violinist, was nearing fifty years of age, but Miguel, eighteen, didn't fare much better as they gingerly settled together at a table with Bernard, Romello, Kenneth, Benny, James, Donald, Chuck, and Douglas.

"How did it go?" Chuck asked no one in particular.

"Man!" Miguel said, expressively. "I hurt in places I didn't know I had."

"It's like that until you learn how to crouch bending your knees."

"I wanted to stand straight," added Fenster, "but it's not a good idea because you have to shift your weight from side to side to steer and avoid people and other obstacles in your path, like trees."

"I kept ending up on my butt and had a hard time trying to figure out how to get up again," commented Gregory.

Everyone laughed.

"Yeah, me, too," said Fenster. "However, I have to admit once I got the hang of it, I had a great time on the bunny runs. I was never athletic as a boy or young man. Miguel and I might go to a batting cage or hit a few tennis balls, but this is extreme for me. I can't imagine flying down one of those big slopes like I saw you guys doing today. Your children were handling the mountains like pros!"

Kenneth, Benny, Donald, Chuck, and James laughed and told funny stories about their early experience on the slopes.

"We brought the children to ski as soon as they could walk," said Kenneth of himself and his offspring.

"When Derrick and his family moved from Philadelphia to Monroe County near us, he and I used to do cross-country skiing in the Poconos more than downhill, but like Gregory, our basketball schedules got in the way. We also had clauses in our contracts prohibiting any activity that might lead to injury. When we switched to medicine, we made time to ski when we went home to visit our families. Derrick built his chalet and invested in this resort because he loved the sport so much. We would come out here as soon as the snow fell and kept coming back every chance we got. I'm glad Vivian decided to keep it for the families' use. My family and Derrick's will be here for a few weeks at Christmas this year, and so will Vivian and I unless our baby comes early in the next week or two."

"JeNelle and I plan to take our children, her parents, her sister, Gloria and David and their family to Lake Tahoe for Christmas this year. What are you and Donald doing, James?"

"We're going to California. Cecile and Janice want to visit their families in Los Angeles, so we're heading out there until after New Year's. My parents are coming, too."

"What about you, Gregory?"

"I'll be in DC with Miguel and Angelique."

"Stacy and I will be in DC with the children, too, for a working vacation until after the New Year. Then we'll head back to Japan," added Benny.

"That's great, Benny. I think Bill will be back from Europe soon."

"Maybe this threat to Angelique will be over by then," commented Fenster.

"Let's hope," said Gregory, noncommittally, but his words lacked conviction.

"It's worse than you've said, isn't it?" asked Miguel.

"Not necessarily worse, just more complicated," Gregory answered.

"Tell us, Gregory. I don't want my Anna blindsided," said Fenster, concerned for his wife, Miguel's and Angelique's mother.

"She won't be. I've taken care of the financial difficulties..."

"She was also in financial trouble?" Fenster questioned, concerned.

"Some."

"If it's about money, I'll cover anything she's lost," offered Miguel.

"I will too," said Fenster.

"Calm yourselves. I've put a plan in play which should bring in enough investors to see her in the black within six months. I will keep an eye on her finances for the foreseeable future until she's comfortable handling things on her own. I'm putting one of CTI's accountants on the daily expenses and income, payroll and taxes. She won't have to do it, but she needs to know all of the details so she will better budget for the long run." He didn't mention he would be among her major investors.

"Still, if she needs anything..."

"I'll let both of you know if she does."

"Thank you, Gregory. I can't express my gratitude strongly enough for everything you've done for Angelique."

"Ditto," said Miguel.

"All right, posse, let's head 'em up and move 'em out," said Chuck. "We can get a few more runs in at night."

"You youngsters go right ahead. Bernard, Romello, and I are heading for the ski lodge to scare up some poker players," said Fenster. "That's something I haven't found time to do in many years. I may break the bank, but I won't break my neck," he said, laughing.

They gathered the children who had eaten their fill at the all-you-can-eat, buffet-style restaurant and were ready and eager for the nighttime ski down the lighted slopes.

Chapter 15

It was nearing eight at night when Gregory and Angelique stopped by Mrs. Joyner's flat to deliver Dejon and Keaton. The boys were still bubbling with stories of all of their exploits in the past ten days since they left New York. They raved about flying in a jet Aretha piloted and taking turns sitting in the co-pilot's seat. Excitedly, they talked all over each other about all the people they met in Gregory's family, the food they ate, the games they played, and the horses they rode. They glowed about going skiing in Colorado; a surprise trip Gregory had not previously told them about. Dejon reminisced about Gregory's beautiful nieces and had his grandmother hooting in laughter. The boy was truly smitten with the young girls in the family. Keaton, the one who usually spotted the pretty women, was waxing eloquent about the horse he got a chance to ride every day and the other farm animals he saw. Rather than grousing about having to get up early to gather eggs for breakfast, the boys were enthusiastic because they got a chance to feed the animals and milk the cows. They even enjoyed taking the morning jog with Gregory and Aretha.

Since they enjoyed skiing so much, Gregory promised to take them to Pennsylvania or Vermont during the Christmas break to ski. He was also looking into local ski clubs for their age groups. For Keaton, he would find out about riding lessons.

By the time Gregory and Angelique prepared to leave and walk the rest of the way home carrying their duffels, the boys were e-mailing his young family members continuing the fast friendships they made over the Thanksgiving holiday. Mrs. Joyner was appreciative of the free time and, smiling, said she and Mr. Conway were planning a third date. She thanked Angelique profusely for putting them together. Their first date had been lunch at a nice restaurant in Harlem and the second date, dinner and an off-Broadway show on Thanksgiving Day. She looked forward to her third date.

"Did you have a good time?" Gregory asked, as he reset the alarm in his home before climbing the steps. They placed their duffels by the stairs, shed their coats, and settled in Angelique's favorite spot overlooking the beautifully lit bridges. Gregory poured a couple of goblets of wine before handing one to her and settling down beside her on the window seat.

"Always. I really enjoy being with your family. Your cousin, Satarah, is an amazing woman raising six children and running a busy business at the same time. All of the women in your family are like that though, especially Vivian."

"They are, yes. All of them are phenomenal women in their own way." Especially his mom, he thought privately.

"I really liked how the children did set-up and then cleaned up after dinner. Then the men served the coffee and desserts."

"It's a relatively new tradition. I usually couldn't make it home for Thanksgiving before because I was either in training or on the road for exhibition games, but my dad instituted the tradition of the men serving the women."

"I think it's a sweet gesture. Was the ski trip fun?"

"It was, yes, after I learned how to stay on my feet for more than five seconds," he said, smiling and took a sip of his wine.

"I've never been skiing, but Fenster and Miguel said they also enjoyed it. They're both looking forward to next year."

"I am too, but I plan to take the boys skiing over the holidays and maybe several weekends a month after that. By this time next Thanksgiving, we'll be able to ski the more challenging runs with my family." He relaxed comfortably into the seat. "It's rare I could get together with my brothers and cousins," he said, smiling at the thought. "We used to do it every summer for Labor Day at great-grandaunt Hanna

Ivy's home in Atlantic Beach before we headed back to high school, college or grad school. The young cousins still carry on the summer's end reunion tradition. My great-grandaunt is reaching her nineties, but she loves to have the family come each year. We would camp out on the beach in tents and sleeping bags in her yard, which happened to be on the shore of the Atlantic Ocean. We'd be up with the sun every day. Of course, our great-grandaunt saw us as a source of cheap labor to paint walls, scrub windows and floors, and run errands," he said, laughing. "She and her senior friends sat around on the veranda sipping mint juleps and playing cards while they worked us like Georgia mules." His smile broadened at the memory.

"She seems so spry still."

"Oh, she is, yes. She still goes swimming several times a week at the local YWCA."

"She never married or had children?"

He took another sip of wine. "No, she was a Nurse Practitioner, the youngest of her eleven siblings, and took care of my mother, her siblings, and cousins when their parents, her siblings, my maternal grand and great-grandparents were touring the country with the great Josephine Baker and in Europe putting on musical shows to support the family. When all the children in my mother's generation were out of high school and off to college she was already in her fifties. Great-grandaunt, Hanna Ivy, became a companion, to a wealthy elderly spinster who had no relatives. The woman left her estate to Aunt Hanna Ivy. As a part of the inheritance, she owned two houses; the one she sold to my brother, Benny, where you used to live in Georgetown and the one in Atlantic Beach where she still lives now. She preferred the milder weather in the south to the colder north."

"She told me she's leaving the house at the beach in her will as a family trust."

"I know, yes. She wants it to always be available for the family's use and asked whether I might want to move there as the trust manager. I have other ideas I plan to implement within the next few months, for example, chartering a South Carolina state bank. Living in South Carolina would be ideal for that purpose and managing a new professional development league I and some other former players are going to start. It's a semi-pro basketball league in the Mid-Atlantic States of Virginia, Maryland, North Carolina, South Carolina and Washington, DC. I'm also considering a contract offer to do the play-by-play or color commentary for certain NBA games."

Stunned, she just stared. "Would you do it? I mean would you move back to South Carolina?"

"I would, yes. I'm still young enough to need interesting challenges in my life. I moved to New York because I signed with a New York basketball team and ultimately because I wanted to trade on the big board, but I never intended to make it my permanent home. I'm essentially a southern, country boy. Technology is so advanced now I don't have to be in the city to work at my firm. We live in a virtual reality world. I can do what I do from anywhere. I like the idea of living at the beach in the south year-round and coming to New York only when I have to. I also want to build a home in Goodwill on land I inherited from my paternal great grandparents just as Kenneth, Benny, and Vivian have done. So have my cousins Donald and James Dixon and others. We share the same great-grandparents who provided for all of us in their wills. The Grand Strand is only an hour or so drive from Goodwill. I like the idea of spending more time at home with my parents, cousins, and aunts and uncles"

"Then you're going to take your great grandaunt up on her offer?"

"Probably, but not for a few years yet. I can handle my projects in South Carolina from here for a while. I've already contracted with JaiHonnah and JRock to design and build my home in Goodwill beginning in the spring of next year, but I want to see Dejon and Keaton graduate from high school and go to college before I leave the city."

"They're thirteen and eleven now. College isn't that far off for them."

"It's not, no. Six years; seven at the most. By next year the development league and my bank should be up and operational. I'll trade on the big board during the week and spend the weekends sportscasting."

"What about this place? You've built an impressive home here."

"I won't sell this home. I'll come back here when I need to be in the city, but I will make South Carolina my permanent residence either at the beach or in Summer County."

"You're telling me this because I want you to father my baby."

"If I were to do something like that, Angelique, you would be my wife and any decision about where we lived would be made jointly. I will not father a child out of wedlock and I will father a child only with someone who I'm in love with and who is in love with me. Someone I intend to spend the rest of my life with. We've only been back in each other's lives for a short period of time. I need time to ensure what I feel for you is not just momentary heat. Frankly, threatening to be artificially inseminated doesn't convince me you're ready for the type of relationship I want to offer a woman I would marry."

His naked honesty shamed and humbled her. "I shouldn't have done it."

He swallowed the last of his wine and placed his and her empty goblets on the coffee table. "No, you shouldn't have." Caressing her face and seeing the obvious need for him in her eyes was the most physically gratifying sexual experience he had in some time. He drew her to him and kissed her mouth with rampant carnality, causing an avalanche of soul-shuddering sensations. He broke the kiss, his forehead to hers. Closing his eyes to calm himself, he said, in a caressing voice, "Don't misunderstand, Angel. I do want to make love with you, but not unless or until we're further along in our relationship to know where we're going." He stood and helped her up from the window seat. "Now go to bed, Angel, before I forget my resolve to keep my hands off of you."

Understanding he was making an effort toward a relationship and he was not a man who could be pressured or manipulated, she rose on her toes and briefly kissed him. "Good night, Greg. Sleep well."

As if he could after she raised his body temperature adding heat to lust. He had the presence of mind to turn on his bedroom light via his hand-held remote unit should someone still be monitoring their activities.

He knew he was not yet ready for bed. At a minimum, he needed to soak in his Jacuzzi to ease the muscle strain in his arms, legs, and thighs or go for a swim. That morning he, Miguel, Dejon, and Keaton joined his family members on slightly more challenging ski runs. He had to admit he enjoyed it, but his body was still acclimating to the new body stresses.

Steam rose from the swimming pool sufficient to coat the glass and turn it opaque. Gregory took off his terrycloth robe and dove into the warm waters at the deep end. The underwater lighting was sufficient enough to see his course. After thirty laps his muscles were beginning to relax. By fifty he was too exhausted to do more. Climbing out of the pool he stretched out on one of the chaise lounges and reflected on the week they spent in Summer County. As he predicted, his family members believed bringing Angelique home was a statement of his intension to marry her. Instead he was continuing to perpetrate the false image they were really a couple. However, he was beginning to believe it himself.

Angelique was ever-present in his thoughts. The trip to Goodwill had been good for her to get out of the house and mix and mingle with family and friends without fear of having her security breached. Her parents and Miguel were already there at his parents' house when they arrived with Aretha, Dejon and Keaton. His parents' home had seven bedrooms, five baths and a half baths, and easily accommodated the extra visitors. His parents were always awake early spending quality time together before the rest of the house stirred.

Since Thanksgiving would be held at The Summer House there wasn't that rushed week of preparations which usually preceded any large family gathering. He did his part gathering fresh fruits, vegetables, and flowers from the hydroponics farms, but Angelique was with him most of the time enjoying herself even if it was labor-intensive. Still, they had time for long walks alone together during the weekend and week before turkey day. They visited family members, enjoying the close comradery he missed in previous years. He liked how easily she and her family fit in with his, especially with one of his favorite female cousin's, Satarah, his Aunt Mariah's younger daughter.

Though they were coming to the cuisine from different perspectives, Angelique and Satarah were able to blend their talents and prepare with Anna's help a feast which had the family sated and raving.

Still, as he relaxed beside the pool, he was no closer to determining what course to take with her in or out of his life.

He had given her a lot to think about, Angelique thought as she prepared for and then climbed into bed. Yes, attempting to coerce him into her bed to father a child with her was not the brightest idea she ever had, but the basic fact was still true. She wanted him as her husband, but she didn't factor in he might have plans which did not include her. He was a man of integrity and thoughtful consideration. She recalled, from an early age, Gregory Clayton Alexander mapped out his future and had not deviated from his plan. He had accomplished the goals he set for himself and was plotting the next steps and stages of his life.

She needed to take a leaf from his playbook and start looking ahead at her own life. Instead of trying to figure out how she could fit into his life, she needed to determine what the next steps and stages of her life would be. The reality was her life might not include Gregory.

She turned over in bed on-to her stomach and stacked her hands under her head. Still, he had kissed her. On a soft sigh, she let sleep claim her.

Chapter 16

"Brittany Marsh," the woman answered her phone in a crisp, business-like tone.

"Hello, Brittany, this is Angelique Menendez-Gaza."

"Well, hello, Angel. It's good to hear from you. I suppose you're calling about my invitation to judge the teen fashion show in a few weeks?"

"I am, yes, however, I have a condition."

"Which is what?"

"I know two young boys I'd like you to use as models."

"Well, I don't know. Have they done any stage work before? Do they have a portfolio? Would I know their reps?"

"No, no, and no. They are complete novices, but I can have them prepped before the show. They'll do an exhibition for you and, if you don't think they're adequate, no harm, no foul."

"Is this your bottom line?"

"It is, yes. I'll also waive any and all appearance fees for myself. If you agree, I'll have my agent, Bill Chandler, get in touch with you with my usual contract requirements and for the boys as well."

"All right, have them come to my office this week. I'll bring in the designers who are exhibiting to see what they think as well. My schedule is full, so I'll have to get with you for a specific day and time."

"Good. We'll connect again in a day or so."

"That will work. Thank you for considering this."

"You're welcomed. Goodbye."

Brittany sat for a moment debating whether what she was about to do was the right thing. She was admittedly a dyed-in-the-wool romantic.

She was French, after all, on her mother's side and British on her father's. She loved a Romeo and Juliette star-crossed lover's story, like her parents' story had been. Then, too, Mr. Durant seemed like such a nice man. His British accent, like her father's, was a killer to any woman who followed the exploits of the British Royals. However, Angel had been in the society columns a lot lately with the sports guy, Greg Alexander. He was certainly a handsome man, but Mr. Durant was British Royalty. He didn't have to be handsome.

In the end, she placed the call. He praised her profusely and promised her a private tour of Buckingham Palace the next time she was in London.

"Yes, I spoke with the agents for the fashion show. Apparently, they are very impressed with what they saw of the Joyner brothers at the exhibition last week. They have some catalog work they want to use them for," Bill Chandler said. "I've looked over your contract and the ones for Dejon and Keaton Joyner. One of my staff attorneys prepared it so I'm green lighting the fashion show project and the catalog work."

"Thanks, Bill. I'll contact Brittany Marsh right away to arrange for Dejon and Keaton to do the catalog shoot. I've had them practicing every day after school in preparation for the fashion show. They're both naturals and should do very well."

"You're not going there alone, are you?"

"No, Bill," she said, on a windy sigh, "I'm not. Mrs. Joyner has given written permission as their legal guardian for me to take the boys to their events if she can't. She can't be there, but Gregory will go with us…"

"And your security team?"

"Yes, and my security team. I'll alert them to the addition to the schedule."

"Good. Now how are you holding up otherwise?"

"I'm fine, Bill. You shouldn't worry so much about me."

"It's my job to worry about you and I don't relish the idea of having my butt chewed off again by The Judge."

Angelique laughed. "It's such a cute butt, too."

"Cut it out, delinquent," he said, without heat. "I shouldn't let you socialize with my sister so much. She's a bad influence on you. You were such a sweet, biddable child."

Angelique laughed at his long suffering sigh. "When will you be home?"

"A week, maybe sooner."

"Great! Maybe you'll be here to see what the Joyner brothers can do on the runway."

"I'll let you know. See you soon."

"Okay. Bye, Bill."

They hung up and Angelique breathed a sigh of relief. She was concerned, given the current circumstances, he would turn down the invitation for her to appear. That would have been a shame if she and the boys had worked so hard for nothing. She put in a call to Brittany confirming the time and a location in the store for the rehearsal before the show and the date and time for the catalog shoot. Then she dutifully alerted her security team about the updated schedule.

"All done?" Gregory asked, as he looked up from his desk near the kitchen area. He had managed to put in a substantial amount of work that day. He found it wasn't debilitating at all to have someone—Angelique—in his home while he worked. She made herself as unobtrusive and inconspicuous as possible, but he did like that she used him as her guinea pig while she worked on her cookbook.

"Yes, Bill gave my appearance a green light and the boys have contracts to do the fashion show and catalog work. He should be home soon." She came, sat on his lap, side saddle, and put her arms around him. She rested her head beside his. "He still won't let me go back to work at my restaurant until this threat is completely over and done. He said maybe I can go back after New Year's."

"Is that so bad?"

"It's not, no. I mean I'm learning how to handle the business and business is really good even without me being there. I'm making progress on my cookbook. I should be ready to show it to your cousin, Jasper Cooper. As an editor with Titan Canadian Book Publishing House, he thinks it will be a top seller on the international market." She framed her hands as a banner. *"WHAT A FASHION MODEL KNOWS ABOUT MAKING MEALS WILL KEEP YOU SLIM AND HEALTHY.* We talked about it during the Thanksgiving dinner. I just need maybe thirty more recipes before I prepare the dishes for the photo shoot. I know who I want to use as the photographer. My friend and fellow super model, Ardon, has been shooting some great photos. If she's willing, I'm going to ask her to do the art work. I'm also thinking about doing a video edition. These will all be gourmet recipes for the busy professional which can be done in thirty minutes or less. Would you be my test subject to see whether you can follow my recipes and prepare them in thirty minutes?"

He shrugged. "Sure. Who else are you going to use?"

"Margo and Joyce, of course."

He laughed. "Joyce will probably be able to do it, but Margo doesn't know what a kitchen is. For her boiling water would be a challenge."

She also laughed. "Nevertheless, she agreed to do it."

"Okay, but don't ask me to taste anything Margo cooks."

"Speaking of cooking, what would you like for dinner tonight?"

"We're not eating in tonight."

"Oh, we're not? I thought we didn't have anything on the agenda today."

"We have reservations for a dinner cruise around Manhattan Island so put on some glad rags and we'll head out for dinner and dancing."

"Did you alert the security team?"

"I did, yes. Everything's been taken care of."

"Okay," she said, jovially as she hopped up off his lap and headed up the steps. She had just the dress in mind to WOW him. It was one she bought while shopping with her security team.

Angelique watched Gregory descending the stairs and thought, not for the first time, he would have been a world-class model ranking up there with the likes of Sean O'Pry, Element Chabenaud, Bill Chandler, Matthew Terry, Benjamin Eiden, Arthur Gosse and her brother Miguel. He would have made Vogue, Lacoste, Calvin Klein, Coach and Gucci even wealthier. He had a natural walk which was light, like his feet barely touched the ground. He moved with the sensual confidence of a very successful man. Yet he was solidly built without an ounce of extra meat on his well-toned body. He had an excellent body for men's sportswear, but he killed in formal dress. Her imagination soared with visions of what she wanted to do with and to him intimately.

He was fitting his watch on his wrist as he descended the stairs and hadn't looked up until he reached the last step. When he did, his breath backed up in his throat. *"WOW!"* he exclaimed.

That was just the right reaction she was hoping for. He had a stunned, appreciative stare so she did her signature 360-degree turn as if she were a robotic manikin pivoting on the balls of her feet without appearing to move a muscle. "You like?"

He wanted to say he loved, but thought better of it. "Uh, I'm a guy and I have a pulse . . . or at least I did before I saw you in this . . . uh, dress?"

She smiled brilliantly as he moved toward her and then took her in his arms. "You are absolutely breath-taking, Ms. Menendez-Gaza."

"Thank you, Mr. Alexander," she said, and kissed him.

"We'd better go. I don't trust my chances of remaining celibate when you look like this."

When they walked out of the door, a long, white limo was on the parking pad. The chauffer got out and opened the rear door. Angelique was awed, to say the least, when she climbed in and found bunches of beautiful flowers in stationary holders. They took the short ride to the dock where the dinner cruises were moored.

Yet, when they left the warmth of the limo, Gregory steered her to a different cruiser which was well over one hundred feet long. A white-jacketed man who wore a captain's cap welcomed them aboard. The ramp was immediately removed once they were securely on the deck.

Angelique thought it curious they seemed to be the only dinner guests on board, but the chilled night air carried the scent of cuisine native to Peru, causing her appetite to engage.

They stood on the forward deck while the boat left the dock and got underway. The night was clear and cool, the breeze frisky and playing havoc with her upswept hairdo with loose tendrils around her shoulders. Gregory stood at her back, his hands on the rails on each side of her to secure her as the boat picked up cruising speed.

"Beautiful," she said, looking at the brightly lit buildings and nighttime cityscape on both sides of the Hudson River.

"I'll say," Gregory said, looking at her profile and not the scenery.

She smiled bashfully. People thought her to be beautiful, but she didn't feel it until Gregory looked at her in the special way he did.

"Mr. Alexander?" a ship's steward interrupted.

"Yes?"

"If you'll follow me, all is ready."

"Thank you," he said, and guided Angelique to the entrance of the main cabin.

Just after they entered flashlights began popping on and illuminating faces she recognized. Voices began singing "Happy birthday." When all of the lights grew in intensity the cabin came alive with people she held most dear. Her hands went to her mouth in stunned silence. After ponderous moments, she finally found her voice. "I completely forgot it's my birthday."

"It's a good thing you have us around to remind you," said Melissa Charles Lightfoot, her Rhode Island accent strong, her blue eyes shining warmly with her Native American husband, Alan Lightfoot, by her side. They were both part of the housemates' crew who helped to raise her and Miguel and now both were practicing attorneys in Vivian's law firm. With their two sons and baby daughter, they lived across the street from where they used to live when they were both students in the scholars program at Georgetown Law.

Next came David and Gloria Towson Carter, also both former housemates, and Vivian's law partners, who now lived within walking distance of the US Congress. They had three daughters and another baby on the way. Because of Vivian's judgeship, David was the law firm's managing partner. He was also the president of the United States Bar Association.

Bringing up the rear was none other than William Anthony Chandler, Esq., and his sister, Margo "You didn't really think we'd let your twenty-first birthday pass unnoticed, did you?" asked Bill.

"I just talked with you and asked you when you were coming home," she said, while hugging Margo.

"I told you a week or sooner. I decided to make it sooner. Happy Birthday, Angel."

One person after another surprised her. Her parents, Miguel, Vivian and Chuck, Aretha and her longtime man friend, Russell Greene, the young, world-renowned artist, Gregory's parents and siblings, Kenneth and JeNelle, and Benny and Stacy. There was her staff from Angelique's Place and The Run Way handling the food prep and the drinks under her mother's watchful eye and enjoying the music provided by a combo and group she and Gregory had seen and heard perform recently at their album release party. The head of the record label was there with Gregory's business partner China McAllister. She got a big bear hug from Peter Callaway and Joyce Montgomery. The biggest surprise was her friend and fellow super model, Ardon. They hugged like long-lost, sorority sisters.

"Oh, it's so good to see you!" Angelique exclaimed.

"It's been too long. The last time was at your farewell appearance more than six months ago. I've missed you on the circuit."

"I miss the people I care about, but not the grueling schedule, the dieting or the pins getting stuck in me like I was a pin cushion."

"I know what you mean, but I've been dying to ask who is the gorgeous male model escorting you tonight? I haven't seen him before on the circuit. I certainly would have remembered if I had."

"He's a civilian. That's Gregory Alexander."

"You're kidding! He's the one you used to talk about all the time? I'll have to tell Dolce & Gabbana there's a man who wears one of their originals better than anyone who's currently under contract to model for them!"

"He is just this side of perfection, isn't he?"

"And then some. Anymore at home like him?"

"That's his brother, Kenneth, over there," she pointed out.

"WOW!"

"And his other brother, Benny, over there."

"Double *WOW*, they're gorgeous hunks, but they're both wearing wedding bands."

"Yes, they're married to the two women talking with Chandler. The one on the right is JeNelle, Kenneth's wife. She's a US Senator. The other one is Stacy, Benny's wife. She's a Navy Officer."

Ardon turned and looked at the women in question talking with the male phenom whose stage name was Chandler. "Oh, hell," she lamented. "I can't compete with either of them."

They laughed together. "Let me introduce you to Troy Jackson, Adam Atterly, Jeremy Lightfoot, and especially Jackson Chase. They are all drop-dead gorgeous, but more importantly, they're solid, unattached, and available."

"My *sustantivo bebé*, she looks happy, no?" Anna asked.

"I think she's happy. She wasn't expecting this. The birthday party is a complete surprise."

"She is happy because you are looking out for her. You always have. You are a good man, Gregory. Your *momi* and *popi*, they raised you right."

"Thank you, Ms. Anna. I will continue to look out for Angelique. I want only good things for her."

"She is having strong feelings for you."

"I for her as well."

"I know. I love my Angel, but she is young, yet she is a woman. Have a care with your heart. We must leave tomorrow to go back for my husband's tour. Miguel will come with us for a while, but we will be home for Christmas and the New Year. You will come and bring my Angel with you. You will stay with us, yes?"

He kissed her temple and hugged her. "I will bring her, Ms. Anna, but Benny and Stacy will be in Washington, too, so I will stay with them and my nieces and nephews. That's just next door to your home so I'll see you all the time. Now, may I have this dance?"

Angelique watched first Gregory and her mother, and then Mr. Conway and Mrs. Joyner dancing. They seemed blissfully happy or maybe she was projecting her happiness on everyone in the ship's cabin. It took her a-while, but then she realized the cruiser belonged to Vivian. In fact, it was the yacht her first husband, Derrick Jackson, named *The Vivian Lynn* before they were married. Vivian had other ships in her Adventurer Transportation System, but *The Vivian Lynn* she used only for family. It gave Angelique a warm, all-encompassing feeling of belonging.

She had been on the yacht several times and realized the interior was renovated and remodeled. She didn't recognize it when they boarded because it was dark on the dock and her thoughts were filled with Gregory.

"A penny for your thoughts," said Bill.

"I just realized this is Vivian's yacht."

"It is. At Gregory's request, she had it brought up from DC while you were in South Carolina for Thanksgiving."

"How long has Gregory been planning this party?"

"Oh, I'd say from the first night you spent in his home. He wanted to do something to help you feel better. Apparently, you told him you had never been on a dinner cruise around Manhattan. I mentioned you had a birthday coming up, one thing led to another, and, as they say, the rest is history. Come on and dance with me, Angel."

She did and hugged him fiercely.

"So are you seriously still hung up on the age difference?" Vivian asked.

"That and a few other things," said Gregory.

"Need I remind you Derrick was more than twelve years older than me and Chuck is nine years my senior?"

"It was never an issue for you because you've always been mature beyond your chronological age. You're beyond aggressive. You're tenacious and have to know and understand everything and everyone in your orbit. That's why you're a great judge."

She laughed without mirth. "Yet I've made some colossal mistakes."

"If you're thinking about Carlton Andrews, forget about it," he said, with a great Jersey accent. She chuckled at his effort. "If there had never been a Carlton Andrews in your life, you may not have been emotionally prepared to handle someone like Derrick. It would have meant there would not have been any of my beautiful nieces and handsome nephews in your life. Still, if you tell your boys I said they are handsome, I'll deny it."

She laughed at him. "I get your point. It all worked out for the best, but I don't need to tell my boys anything. The girls constantly blow up their cell phones. Just like the girls did when you were my sons' ages. You know what your responsibilities are vis-a-vis your nephews."

"Yes, I know. It's time I have a little heart-to-heart with them."

"They love you, but they have a healthy fear of me and I encourage and perpetuate the emotion."

Gregory snorted derisively. "Yeah, they're not the only ones who fear you."

She grinned malevolently at her younger brother. She rose from her seat beside him. "Give yourself a break, G. I have it on good authority, from the oracle of our family, your sister and mine, you're doing an excellent job of taking care of your responsibilities." She kissed his forehead. "I have to make a pit stop. This new niece or nephew of yours is tap dancing on my bladder." She waddled away.

Chapter 17

"Wow, some night, huh?" commented Angelique, her arms full of flowers.

"It certainly was. Imagine my sister giving birth on her yacht in the middle of the Hudson River. It's right up there with Sully Sullenberger landing his jet on the water."

Angelique beamed a smile causing her eyes to dance with merriment. "Chuck and Vivian named her Teresa Angelique because she was born on my birthday." She deeply sniffed the bunch of flowers in her arms before she began to arrange them in vases Gregory supplied.

"You and I get to be her godparents."

"I'm so excited. Are you sure Vivian is okay?"

"I'm sure. Chuck was right there," Gregory said, leaning his butt comfortably against the counter watching her work magic with the flower arrangements. "After all, he's an emergency room doctor and he's delivered his share of babies. Need I remind you my mother, who is a veteran Registered Nurse, the head of Nursing at Summer County General and the Director of the Nursing School at Summer County Academy was there too and together they were able to deliver little Teresa Angelique Montgomery before midnight?"

"We can go see them in the hospital tomorrow, can't we?"

"You mean today, don't you? If I know my sister, and I do, she'll be out of the hospital in no time. Dad, Bill, and Aretha are going to Maryland to pick up Chuck and Vivian's children and bring them to New York. They'll be here before ten this morning. We're going to have a houseful for a few days until Chuck says Vivian and Teresa can travel."

"I still can't believe it. One minute Vivian went to the restroom and the next thing we know, her water broke and the baby was coming. How cool is that?"

"I couldn't tell you. I'm not a girl, thank The Creator and all of The Ancestors," he deadpanned and had Angelique laughing.

"The baby came fast."

"This wasn't Vivian's first rodeo. She's had several babies before, remember," he said, wryly. "She knows the drill."

"Did I tell you how much I enjoyed my surprise birthday party?"

"Oh, only about a few dozen times."

"Truly, Gregory, thank you for doing this. It was the very best birthday party I've ever had."

"You're welcome. It was your twenty-first, so it had to be special. However, since you didn't get to open your gifts during the party, I thought you might like to open at least one," he said, taking a gaily decorated oblong box from his inside breast pocket and presenting it to her.

She carefully peeled off the beautiful paper to find a Harry Winston box. Inside was an intricately designed lily cluster diamond bangle bracelet with matching drop earrings. She knew this gift to be a one-of-a-kind set from the exclusive jeweler's collection. She also knew it was extremely valuable, but to her as she looked up into Gregory's handsome face, she was helpless to stem the tide of tears running down her cheeks. *He* was her gift, more precious than any valuable stones.

Gregory sensed what the gift meant to her and helped her fasten the bracelet on her wrist. She changed out the earrings she was wearing for the new ones, smiling through her tears. He palmed her face and smoothed away her tears with his thumbs. "Happy birthday, Angel Face."

It brought more tears as she hugged him and buried her face in his chest.

By noon, later that day, laughter, high-pitched squeals, and giggles were bouncing off the walls and high ceilings. Little people were in every nook and cranny of Gregory's home. No matter the number of bodies, there was still ample space for the radio-control car races along one strip of smooth, heated flooring where unnatural obstacles, like plastic cups and water bottles, had been placed on the floor. Ten cars raced through the course bumping into objects and losing points for each crash.

Angelique nimbly stepped out of the way before a car ran over her Prada-clad toes. She reached the kitchen counter without incident where Gregory was setting up a tray of hot dog and hamburger buns straight from the grill.

"Do you have any more relish, Uncle G?" asked Preston, one of Vivian's and Chuck's older boys. He and their other boys, the twins, Ryan and Roger, better known as the Kelso twins, were aiding in the preparation of the lunch-time meal.

"Check the bottom, left shelf in the pantry," Gregory called out over the din. It was a good thing, he thought, he had a high ceiling or the noise and the flying drone-like helicopters would have been crushing and crashing.

It was also a good thing his kitchen space easily accommodated the ten or so cooks and helpers.

Kenny and Kevin, Kenneth and JeNelle's oldest twin boys, were aiding Mrs. Joyner blend what could be described only as a vat of chili with sautéed ground round, ground turkey, celery, peppers, tomatoes and red beans in a huge pot.

"Coleslaw needs a little more mayo," yelled Kenneth's and JeNelle's Justin. His twin, Jarrett, went to the pantry with their cousin, Brian, pulling out the mobile shelving units to locate another container.

Dejon and Keaton clambered up the steps from the ground floor carrying large bowls of freshly picked strawberries and grapes, followed by Kenneth's and JeNelle's twin girls Marcella and Michelle. They snaked their way to the trestle table avoiding collisions with escaping smaller people toddling by on short legs intent on a kick-the-balls game.

"Did you wash the fruit?" Gregory asked.

"We did, Uncle G," answered Michelle.

Aretha continued making the fruit, assorted cheese, and cracker trays with the arrival of the children's harvested bounty.

Bernard cored and then cut fresh pineapple into wedges and added it to a similar stack ready to be grilled by his son. No sooner than he finished the last one, Benny lifted the tray and danced nimbly around his triplet sons, Thomas, Alvin, and Andre, who were intent on playing with a train set on a low, wide, square, soft-edged coffee table.

Whitney Ivy and Linda were on diaper duty and patrol with the youngest of the children still not quite potty-trained.

Whitney's triplet sisters, Shannon, Sharon, and Sierra, were challenging their cousins, Geneva, Vincent, and Dena, to a Wii baseball game on the big screen near the back of the expanse.

Chuck and Vivian's children, Craig, Petra, Reed, and Stephany, were coming down the stairs from setting up the cots and sleeping bags while Micah, Derrick, Jr., and Spencer were coming up the steps from the garage level after shooting baskets. They were a part of the cleanup crew so they got out of the way until they were needed.

"What needs doing, Uncle G?" Derrick, Jr., called out as he snitched a piece of fruit from the pile his grandfather had saved for himself.

Gregory looked around and stopped when his eyes passed over Angelique who was teaching several of his nieces how to fold napkins into what looked like birds taking flight or origami. She just seemed to fit in with the cavalcade of blended family members.

"Uncle G?" Derrick, Jr., Vivian's first and only natural-born son with her late husband, called out again.

"Bring up the tables and chairs from the storage room," instructed Gregory.

"Got it," said Spencer as the four strapping youngsters headed back downstairs to the lower level. Shortly, round tables were wheeled off of the elevator followed by folding chairs. Susannah, Ronnie, and Stanley went to lend a hand with the set-up grabbing tablecloths from below the window seat as they went.

If there was work to be done, Gregory thought, his nephews and nieces didn't have to be asked. They just stepped up to do whatever came next. It's what came of good home training. Greg took a moment to look around and appreciate *whose* he was. His parents were the hub and every offspring vital to the family collective. His father sat cutting more fruit, green and red apples this time, and talking with his grands. Gregory's brothers, Kenneth and Benny, had been in the garage with several of their children working on the old cars. Their wives, JeNelle and Stacy, were playing board games with some of the children. His mother and Chuck were at the hospital checking on Vivian and Teresa. His Angelique was still sitting at the kitchen bar teaching a group of his nieces and nephews how to fold napkins to look like flowers or birds.

The chaos was somehow tranquil.

After lunch they hopped on the subway to McCoy's Department Store to do some shopping and see how imaginatively the windows were dressed for Christmas. Then they toured Manhattan to check out the windows of Bergdorf Goodman, Bloomingdale's, Henri Bendel, Lord & Taylor, Macy's, and Saks, making a loop and ending at Rockefeller Center to ice skate on The Rink and see the big Christmas tree. They had dinner at Angelique's Place before heading out to the theatre for the eight o'clock performance of the Nutcracker Suite with Chuck and Vivian's Linda, in the starring role.

Later that night after the Broadway show, it was a good thing the cots were already set up when they got back to Gregory's home because the crew was worn out. The little ones were bathed and put to bed first. Then the rest showered and turned in.

Gregory and Angelique sat talking with his parents, Kenneth and JeNelle, Aretha and Russell, and Benny and Stacy.

"Vivian's coming home tomorrow," said Sylvia Alexander of her daughter.

"Chuck went back to the hospital already to spend the night with them," mentioned Stacy.

"We'll go to the hospital after breakfast," said Bernard. "The press and news media have gotten wind of Teresa Angelique's arrival and are clamoring for a photo op."

"Somehow they have pictures of her already," said Aretha. "So I posted the details for the rest of our family on my blog."

"Good. Maybe this will take some of the hype out of the press," said JeNelle.

"You've had to deal with more than most because Kenneth was the California governor for eight years and you're a US Senator."

"We have, yes, and we're pregnant again. After the first of the year, I'll be launching my reelection campaign for the US Senate," said JeNelle.

"Then my new niece or nephew will be born in the middle of your campaign."

"Babies," said Kenneth. "We know we're having at least two, maybe even three."

Sylvia laughed, delighted. "Wow, Bernie and I really dodged the probability of multiple births. It skipped our generation and landed on our offspring. Well, with the exception of Bernie's sister, Olivia, and her husband, Romello. They have twins, Donald and James, and both of them have at least one set of twins. Both sides of our family have twins and triplets in abundance."

"Mine, too," said JeNelle. "My mother is a twin and so was her father, my maternal grandfather."

"We have the same high probability in my family," said Stacy. She looked at her younger brother, Russell, and grinned. "I'm a twin and my maternal grandmother had two sets of twin boys. Benny and I have already had two sets of triplets. We're betting with the frequency of multiple births in his and mine, we will likely continue the trend," she said, laughing at her brother's fear-ridden face.

Russell looked at Aretha who also just grinned. He palmed his face, shook his head, and moaned, "Oh, hell."

Everyone laughed at his antics. He was in his mid-twenties and he and Aretha were nowhere near ready for a commitment which would include marriage and babies.

"I'm surprised Vivian and Chuck haven't had twins or triplets," said JeNelle.

"Well, they have adopted four sets of twins."

"That's because in some more primitive cultures, twins born joined together are considered a bad omen. In many of those communities the children are immediately given up for adoption. Of course, the medical costs are staggering when it comes to separating conjoined twins."

"Chuck and his hospital specialize in the procedures necessary to separate conjoined twins. That's why they have so many sets of twins. Even after the successful medical procedure, the biological parents don't want the babies returned."

"Well, not until someone mentioned to Vincent's and Geneva's biological parents how wealthy Chuck and Vivian are. Then they sued for custody and millions of dollars in child care cost," Sylvia said, annoyed.

"Now, hon, stop fretting about it," consoled her husband, Bernard. "David handled the case brilliantly and the parents got nothing, not even visitation."

"It scared Vincent and Geneva," she fussed. "They were under three months old when Derrick and Vivian adopted them and still too young to remember Derrick before he died. The idea they could be taken away from the only parents and family they have ever known terrified them. I will never forgive those people for doing that to my grandbabies just for the money they were after."

"They're thirteen years old now and had been in an orphanage for some time with medical problems. No one wanted to adopt them together because of the extraordinary cost of taking care of them, but Derrick had been donating his time and medical service to the orphanage and was very attached to his infant patients. When Vivian suggested they adopt several of his patients, he didn't hesitate."

"I wish he could see how happy and healthy all of the children he and Vivian adopted or planned to adopt are now."

"I have to trust and believe he watches over them and the children Vivian and Chuck continue to save and adopt."

"On that pleasant thought, I think we'll turn in," said Kenneth, as he and JeNelle rose from their seats. The others followed suit, hugging and kissing each other goodnight.

"Are you running in the morning?" asked Kenneth.

"Six-thirty," said Gregory.

"I'll join you," Kenneth said.

"Stacy and I will too," said Benny.

Stacy Alexander had secretly trained twelve other military women she handpicked as Navy SEALs and Mossad operatives. For years they conducted covert operations worldwide, often in dangerous or life-threatening situations. She was now an Admiral, an integral advisor to the President's Joint Chiefs of Staff, and still, from time to time, conducted covert ops with those she trained or directed operations at the behest of the super-secret organization known only as The Nursery.

No one in her family or Benny's save one knew the extent of her involvement in upholding national and world security. The fact she, Benny, and their children were in country from Japan early for an extended period was calculated to coincide with the threat to Angelique and what she, her other operatives, and Slade Richardson learned was a threat to others as well. She had asked to be read into the operation because the threat involved her husband's family; a family she had easily come to love fiercely and by extension the extended family members as well.

"I'll have breakfast started when you return," said Sylvia. "Janie Joyner said she'd come and help since her grand boys stayed here tonight and need to be off to school early in the morning.

"Since I'm not running with the pack," said JeNelle, rubbing her baby bump, "I'll help in the kitchen."

Angelique didn't think she could sit still for another second. She kept looking at the over-sized clock on the kitchen wall and trying to listen to hear when a car pulled onto the parking pad out front. It was nearly half two in the afternoon and except for her and Mrs. Joyner, everyone else had gone to the park. She was supposed to be basting the hams and checking on the large slabs of roast beef slowly turning on spits in the wall ovens for tonight's dinner, but Vivian was coming home at any minute bringing Teresa Angelique with her. It seemed to Angelique, hours earlier Bernard and Sylvia Alexander left the house to meet Chuck at the hospital and pick up Vivian and her daughter when in point of fact it was just after lunch. Shortly thereafter, everyone, except her, had dressed to take a long walk in the snowy weather which greeted them that morning. She wanted to be here to greet her godchild.

She looked out the window toward the river. It was still snowing heavily and according to the weather report, they were in for a Nor'easter. Flights were being canceled and traffic was snarled, but it was still a pretty sight to see the big, white, fluffy snowflakes falling.

"Mind the soup now, Ms. Angel," Mrs. Joyner cautioned.

"Oh!" Angelique exclaimed, hopping up from her perch on a tall chair at the nine-foot long and wide quartz breakfast bar. She grabbed a pot holder on her way to the stove to stir the vegetable soup she made using fresh ingredients and herbs from Gregory's basement hydroponics farm.

She still had an ample amount of tomato bisque left from what she served with hoagies, dill pickles, and chips for lunch. The fresh field greens salad, Mrs. Joyner's bread loaves with the ham and roast beef, collard greens, green beans, mac and cheese and sweet potatoes would round out the dinner meal. She made three, four-layer sheet cakes after breakfast this morning to serve with the pecan and strawberry ice creams Gregory made in his electric churns. Mrs. Joyner made pumpkin pies as well.

"How about some almonds for those green beans?" suggested Mrs. Joyner.

"I don't know whether anyone has an allergic reaction to nuts. Let's go with the pearl onions and chopped tomatoes instead."

"You're right. Wouldn't want anyone to get sick. My boys don't have that kind of problem. They'll eat most anything."

Angelique smiled distractedly at the woman who was fast becoming a dear friend.

"Now you stop frettin', Ms. Angel. They'll be here by and by."

She shook her head and sighed. "Let me go harvest some more tomatoes."

"Onions, too," Mrs. Joyner advised as Angelique went down the steps. "Might want to bring up some more milk while you're at it. Those babies are going to want hot chocolate when they come in from their hike in the park," she called out, her voice rising.

She was right, Angelique thought. They had plenty of hot coffee and tea, but the children would want cocoa. She filled a rolling cart with more as if she were in a grocery store. Now she understood why Gregory stocked so much in his extra freezers, dry goods, and hydroponics gardens. They had only one more bushel of apples, one of sweet potatoes, and two bushels of fresh corn on the cob left from the ones they had picked up from Mrs. Joyner's church. Greg wanted to try his hand at making apple wine. She smiled to herself. He had an adventurous nature in so many ways and was very creative too. He continued to study things that interested him even to the point of contacting experts in any field of endeavor to ask questions or kick around ideas. His search for knowledge was nearly insatiable. She admired him for it and so much more.

Yet, he took his time with people, especially the ones he cared about. If she had literally thrown herself at some of the men she knew, they would have grabbed what she offered and never taken time to get to know her; to really know the person inside. She hoped Gregory would come to realize she was a woman of simple, uncomplicated needs. She wanted, above all else, to be a wife and mother. She had enjoyed her acting and modeling careers, but in both undertakings she wore a false face. She portrayed someone else. Yes, she could learn her lines for movie roles. She had been cast in such diverse roles as the leading lady in Hiawatha; the female supporting actress in a remake of West Side Story; and one of the angels in the newest movie version of Charlie's Angels. She knew how to sell a fashion designer's line of cosmetics to a camera or a line of clothes to buyers for big department stores. She wasn't impressed by wealth or wealthy people, but she was enthralled by Gregory's intelligence, drive, and ambition. He enjoyed himself, his life and most of all, his family. He was so affectionate with his parents, siblings, nephews and nieces, and by extension his sisters-in-law and brother-in-law.

He was a thoughtful, unobtrusive friend to his partners and a great role model for Dejon and Keaton. He genuinely cared about people which, in her estimation, made him the quintessential phenomenal man. A man who, when she turned around, was leaning against the door jamb studying her, his long, strong legs crossed at the ankle and his arms folded across his broad, firm chest.

She leaned slowly away from the table and silently walked toward him, her eyes intent on his. The chilled outside air was still radiating off of him as she palmed his cheeks, raised on her toes, and took his mouth with a delicious lassitude.

"Hi," she breathed, burying her head and arms inside his LL Bean heavy-duty, weather coat.

"Hi, what were you thinking about?" he asked, cocooning her inside his coat with one arm and palming her head with the other. He released the tie holding her hair in a loose top knot and let it cascade over her shoulders and down her back in a waterfall of silky texture.

"I was thinking about you, the person you are, and why you are who you are."

"Oh," he said, and chuckled while running his finger through her illustrious hair.

"Is everyone back?"

"No, they're out scouring the stores for eggs and milk. Looks like my family will be here for a while. There's at least seven inches of snow on the ground now with a prediction of ten to twelve inches more before midnight. We're going to be snowed in for the next few days. Schools let out early, but I missed Dejon and Keaton before they left. So I came home to get the boys to take them with us."

"Good. You have only two five-gallon jugs of milk left and maybe four dozen eggs."

"I know. I spoke with Mrs. Joyner. She told me what we needed. Mom, dad, and Chuck are shopping at grocery stores and bodegas along the route to here. Fortunately, Chuck was able to score some of the supplies we need from the hospital's storeroom and from your restaurant. Dad says the traffic is so jammed he could probably make better time if he walked here. With the stops along the way, they'll be delayed getting home. How are we doing down here?"

"The strawberries are all gone, but you have blueberries, raspberries, blackberries, and red, green and purple grapes. Not many cantaloupes and honey-dew melons are left. Only one bushel of apples and two bushels of corn are left. I thought I'd make stewed cinnamon apples to go with the ham and corn pudding. There are other vegetables, but not a lot."

"Don't forget I still have food in the freezers down here. Take a look and see what you can do with what's in the storeroom. We should be fine for the next three or four days. I have to bring up more wine and beer for dinner. Almost everyone from your birthday party, except your staff and parents, will be here for a mini-celebration of Teresa Angelique's arrival."

"How are Vivian and Teresa?"

"They're fine, warm, and comfortable in the limo. They were sleeping while dad and Chuck were loading everything they needed for the foreseeable future. Mom is with her. Now that I've got the boys, we're going to get back out there before the stores sell out of the things we need. Do you need more help in the kitchen?"

"No, Mrs. Joyner and I are fine, but because of the extra guests, I think I'll bake some chicken to go with the ham and roast beef and some apple pies."

"Whatever you think is best. There are chickens, parts and turkeys in the freezer, ground beef and pork roasts" he said, and kissed her mouth. "Do you need my help getting this upstairs?"

"I don't, no. You go. Don't keep the boys waiting."

He caressed her face again and was gone.

She sighed and returned to her tasks, adding baked chicken, corn pudding, and apple pies to the menu. Tomorrow they would have roasted turkey with onion bread stuffing.

Dinner over and the clean-up complete, there were people everywhere. They were swimming in the rooftop pool and lounging on the deck, the space completely as warm as a summer day. Even with the snow piled high outside the glass walls, the swimming pool was crowded. The game room was packed and every activity engaged. A basketball game was underway on the garage level while movies, popcorn and pop could be had in the bedroom level's common space. Those who were not engaged in one activity or another were lounging on the main level.

Angelique sat in one space next to Vivian holding eight pound, six ounce Teresa while she slept unaffected by the amount of activity around her. The infant girl was absolutely beautiful, Angelique thought. She had a head full of dark, curly hair, a warm, light-brown complexion, blue eyes, and tiny hands and fingers. One hand strongly latched onto Angelique's index finger and tried to bring it to her rosebud mouth to suckle. Angelique found she couldn't stop touching the baby. She was content to just sit and hold her namesake forever.

She had been on her feet most of the afternoon cooking for over fifty people, but it felt like a vacation as compared to cooking for over six hundred; two hundred for each of three daily seatings. She didn't have to do much more than get out of the way once the food was ready. Capable hands did the setup, prepared the buffets, and cleaned up. She noted only chicken bones went into the trash. Everything else was consumed. Though she couldn't hear them, she knew the two dishwashers were still going at full tilt, but the big pots, pans, and trays were hand-washed and put away by a legion of helpful hands. Except for the ham bones Mrs. Joyner was boiling in one of the crockpots to season more greens and string beans, the kitchen area was clean and tidy.

"That felt good," said Russell Greene as he, Aretha Alexander, and Jackson Chase came down the stairs wearing terrycloth robes and using towels to dry their faces and hair.

"You're right about that, but your nieces and nephews must be only half air-breathing amphibians," said Jackson, laughing. "They have to have gills. They swim like fish."

Chuck laughed. He had one of his female amphibians, Eden, curled in his lap. Until Teresa came along, Eden was the baby of his large crew of offspring. Once he brought the baby home, Eden couldn't take her eyes off of her newest sister. Generally, she would have been in the pool with her siblings, but her attention was riveted to Teresa.

Gregory looked over his family as conversation continued between them, but he had tuned everyone out. He focused on the loving picture Angelique made while holding their god-child. Her hair was thick, pitch black, and loose, falling attractively over her shoulders and down her back. Peace and tranquility were reflected in her face. He could imagine her bringing a child of their making to her breasts to suckle and then making more babies with her. It felt good to think of her in that context; as his wife and the mother of their children. He recognized he was on a slippery slide from lust and heat into being *in love* with Angelique Teresa Menendez-Gaza. He wanted to make promises to her and share her most intimate secrets. Still, it wasn't time yet for that level of commitment, but a strong sensation of contentment passed through him. He had a feeling he would be celibate for some time to come until he believed Angelique would be ready for a lifelong commitment.

Chapter 18

By Friday morning, the house had cleared of all family and visitors. Gregory and Angelique were back to their usual routine, thought Gregory, as he finished an early Saturday morning swim in his rooftop pool. Outside, the temperature was hovering around the twenty degree mark and the streets were still a little too icy to take his usual run around Wall Street or Battery Park.

He had managed to get quite a bit of work done yesterday, some details taken care of for Peter's bachelor party to be held in a private club in Philadelphia, and Peter's and Joyce's wedding scheduled to be held on the Saturday before Christmas. Because the farm where the Montgomerys lived and where the wedding would take place was in a rural area, a helicopter would take the newlyweds to the Philadelphia International Airport to catch an Adventurer Executive Airline jet to Australia. Peter and Joyce would honeymoon there for a month at the ocean-front McCoy Australia Grande. Their penthouse accommodations came complete with catered meals of their choosing and daily housekeeping services. Beyond arranging for Peter's family members to be flown to and from Pennsylvania, Gregory figured his college buddy could handle the rest on his own.

Now, if he could just get a firm grip on what he was going to do about his own life and whether Angelique was going to have a permanent part in it, he could get on track with altered plans for his and her future.

At the moment, Angelique was busy planning a surprise bridal shower to be held at her restaurant at one in the afternoon for approximately fifty of Joyce's female family members and friends. Peter's female family members also would be attending. She hoped the day would go well. It would be the first time she did anything like this, but fortunately crazy Margo and sensible Aretha were lending a hand. Margo secured the services of an all-male dance troupe while Aretha handled the guest lists and logistics of getting everyone who planned to attend there on time.

Angelique had to do only what came naturally. She would handle the venue and the food service.

Margo, Aretha, and she would be the only bridesmaids. They had picked out lovely, Vera Wang sparkling, red dresses for the pre-Christmas wedding event. The wedding gown Joyce would wear was a Carlos Ortega original which would flatter their friend's full figure. The rest of her trousseau was just as exciting, though Joyce had yet to see it. It was Angelique's surprise gift to her long-time friend.

Gregory would stand up as Peter's best man while the other Callaway brothers filled out the roles of groomsmen. Everything was moving fast since they didn't have a lot of time before the big day.

"Are we going to be late?" Gregory asked, as he came to sit next to Angelique as she sat on the window seat; her favorite spot it seemed.

She checked her watch. "No, we're scheduled to be there by eleven o'clock."

"Still, let's get the boys and go. Traffic may be tight getting to the store. It's the Christmas rush that's troublesome."

She closed down her iPad and swung her long, toned legs to the floor. "I guess you're right. This schedule is very tight and I don't want the boys to miss out on this opportunity."

"I'll get them," said Gregory as he went up the stairs to where the boys were playing video games.

Before he returned, the front doorbell rang. They weren't expecting any visitors and Angelique knew better than to open the door without first checking the security camera. When she did, she noted her security team had arrived earlier than expected. However, they frequently changed her routine to keep anyone who might be watching off center.

Soon all six were in a dark-colored SUV with tinted windows headed to the store. They pulled into the loading dock area at the back of McCoy's, a boutique department store more upscale than Neiman-Marcus and got out to go through the service entrance to the elevators. They were walking down a long, non-descript hallway bustling with activity from people wearing costumes of popular characters like Porky Pig, Mickey Mouse, the Big Bad Wolf and others when a woman called Angelique's name. They all turned to see the tall, gorgeous model, Ardon, striding toward them.

"Angelique, what are you doing here?"

"Hello, Ardon, I should ask you the same thing. I agreed to be a judge for the new designers' teen wardrobes."

"So did I. I didn't know any other models were participating as judges," she said, as she fell into step with the group and continued down the hall until they came to a dressing room door.

"Neither did I, but let me introduce you to Dejon and Keaton Joyner. Gregory, you already know and these are my friends."

"You've got quite an entourage," Ardon said, smiling and shaking the young boys' hands.

"We're early, but why don't you join us in my dressing room?" offered Angelique. "The boys have to go. This is their first runway modeling assignment. They should walk the floor to get a feel for the room and space before show-time."

"That's a good idea," said Gregory. "It's good to see you again, Ardon," Gregory said, before ushering the boys away. As unobtrusively as possible, the two agents lead Angelique into a dressing room where her name was stenciled on a card on the door. Ardon's dressing room was right across the hall.

"Wow! Gregory Alexander looks better and better every time I see him. That man knows how to wear clothes!" commented Ardon as she roamed Angelique's dressing room. "You're really a lucky woman."

"Well, Dr. Evan Cain is certainly no slouch. Didn't I see the two of you together in the society pages?"

"I'm in love with him and have been since forever. His family lives next door to my Uncle Harry's house in DC. That's where I grew up."

"Your uncle raised you, right?"

"He did, yes, after my parents and little brother died in a car accident. I was also in the car."

"I remember you telling me about it."

"We became friends because you and Miguel lost your father, too, tragically in a house fire."

"We were what, nine or ten when Chandler introduced us?"

"Probably. I had such a crush on Chandler back then. He's still hot," she said, laughing.

"Yes, I know. My family lived in the same house with him. It's hard to imagine he had to take turns taking out the trash and perform other household duties between modeling assignments when he was still in law school," Angelique said, laughing.

"I loved seeing him when it was his turn to bring you and Miguel to school and then pick you up. I'd bum a ride home every chance I got just to look at him," said Ardon, giggling.

"Those were some fun times."

"We went through private school together and can you believe how long ago we graduated?"

"Now I've retired from modeling and started a new career as a restaurateur."

"I seem to be following in your footsteps and taking my interest in photography more seriously."

"That's great! Are you going to do a show?"

"I am. I'm looking for a New York City gallery where I can exhibit."

"If you want to do an early afternoon show, why don't you consider using my restaurant? The space is unused until we start the set up for the first seating at five. You're welcomed to use it before that."

"It's a great idea. It's certainly in the right location and the space would be perfect."

"I'd also like you to do the photos for my cookbook. Think about it and let me know."

"I will," she said, hugging her friend. "I'm going to call my publicist and see what he thinks."

Angelique wrinkled her nose and Ardon laughed. "You still don't like Dvon Chambers."

"I don't, no. The man gives me the creeps."

Ardon laughed at her expression. "He was dying to represent you and Miguel though."

"I know. Thank goodness for some reason he's afraid of Chandler."

"Oh, he hasn't given up hope. He believes your retirement is a temporary thing you'll soon get over."

"Ha! Fat chance," she said, as she stood and went to the clothes bag hanging on the wall. "This is the extent of my modeling these days. Designers send clothes to me to wear for events like this one." She stepped into the restroom, but kept the door ajar to continue talking while she dressed.

"Me, too. Some of it's good. You're wearing Ortega, I see."

"He's one of my favorites," she called out from the small restroom.

"Mine, too. I'm going to ..." she started, but the door opened to the hallway.

"Damn it!" came the terse comment. "Satin, do you have lock?"

"Copy that. The package is secure, Mata Hari."

"Ten four."

"Roll with it," came another voice. "This one is male."

"She's a civilian!"

"No choice at the moment. Have you got a lock on the perps?"

"They're in the horse costume."

"Got it."

They stood watching the events unfolding.

"Lock on a white van," came an update.

"Stall it. Bait and switch."

"Roger that, Mata Hari."

Moments later they watched the kidnappers pop the hood and get out of the van. Agents carefully opened the rear cargo doors and retrieved the kidnapped woman and substituted another.

"Good job. Now, reinstall and proceed with the op."

"Done. Blue team, you've got the lead!"

"Acknowledged."

"That was close."

"Not something which was unexpected."

Angelique rubbed her temple and then stood up. She could have sworn she had just taken a nap, but the bench in the little bathroom wasn't long enough for it. She shook her head as if to clear it and then checked her face in the mirror. Her eyes were a little irritated, but nothing else seemed awry. She left the bathroom and went into the dressing area.

Wasn't she just talking with Ardon? she wondered. She shrugged off the thought and applied her makeup.

A knock sounded at her door before the stage manager stuck his head inside. "We're ready for you, Ms. Angel."

She stood and took one last look before following him out. Her security team fell into step behind her.

Brittany Marsh did a double take it seemed to Angelique; a rather odd reaction she thought. Still, she was feeling a little odd herself, but continued on to stage left to wait for her cue.

She was joined shortly thereafter by Ardon who also looked a little off center.

"When did you leave?" asked Angelique.

"Leave?" she asked, as if the word was foreign to her.

"Yes, we were talking about the good old days and then . . . ."

"You're up first, Ardon," interrupted Brittany who seemed uncharacteristically nervous.

"Break a leg," offered Angelique.

Ardon gave her a cocky smile and a thumbs-up before strutting onto the stage to rousing applause.

"Uh, Angel, did you and the Earl of Devonshire have a happy reunion?" Brittany asked, her eyes aglow and dreamy.

Angelique looked askance at the woman, narrowing her eyes. "The Earl? You mean Stan Durant?"

"Well, I wouldn't call him ... I mean, I'm just a commoner and he's royalty and all."

"He's here?"

"Well, yes, of course, I thought ... Well he just misses you to pieces, he said ..." she enthused.

"Brittany!" came the terse summon. "Angel's intro has played twice! What's wrong with you?" the stage manager said, annoyed. "You're up, Angel!"

"Thanks," she said, still a little taken aback, but she automatically shifted into model mode and did what came next. She made the sign of the cross and slipped into her robotic manikin personae like a second skin. Her signature tune began and she moved through the curtains. The camera flashes no longer bothered her when she took to the stage and the applause, whistles, and hoots were reminiscent of her many performances. She locked and blocked her movements when the audience came to their collective feet in adoration.

She couldn't see beyond the floor and flood lights, but she could hear Gregory's *"Bravo"* above the din and smiled off in that direction. At the end of the runway, she released her robotic movements, smiled, and waved to the audience before taking her seat with the other judges.

Gregory was enormously proud of Angelique's performance. He had never seen her live on the runway before, but obviously the crowd had and showed their adoration from the moment she appeared on stage. He had to admit it gave him an uncomfortable feeling when the announcer repeated her name twice before she finally took to the stage, but she was the consummate performer. She looked like a manikin with a fixed stare and expression on her gorgeous face, but she moved like a robot without seeming to move a muscle. It was quite an act.

He and the boys had slipped out from backstage just long enough to see her entry. Excitement emanated from the two boys as they were fitted for the first set of clothing of several they would exhibit that day.

They looked confident, promising, after seeing Angelique's performance, they wouldn't let her down. And they didn't. In fact, they individually seemed to mimic her movements almost exactly to the audiences delight. They were a big hit each time they appeared on stage demonstrating a level of professionalism matched by the veteran young models. Their actions seemed to accentuate each outfit they wore.

It was clear to him and to Mrs. Joyner, who had happy tears flowing down her cheeks, Dejon and Keaton were instant hits with the young designers and with the buyers in the audience.

"That was awesome!" proclaimed Keaton as they sat in Angelique's restaurant in advance of the five o'clock seating.

Also at the table were Dejon, Janie Joyner, Ardon, Angelique and Gregory. They were reviewing the photos Gregory and Mrs. Joyner had taken with cell phones and cameras.

"Man! These threads are tight!" exclaimed Dejon.

"You did yourselves proud today," said Mrs. Joyner.

"There are several top designers and agencies who want to put you both under contract," said Ardon.

"Can we like do it again?" asked Keaton.

"You *may*, if your grandmother allows it," said Gregory.

"Grandma?"

"We'll see, Dejon. Gregory suggested I talk with Bill Chandler before I agree to anything."

"He's an excellent agent," added Angelique.

"Everybody talked about him back-stage," said Keaton. "He's like really good, huh?"

"He is, yes," said Gregory. "Since some of the designers want to use you two for the spring and summer lines, we'll talk with Bill later tonight."

"Cool," said Keaton.

"When is your contract up with Dvon?" Angelique asked Ardon. She laughed. "You really want me to switch representation, huh?"
"I do, yes."
She shook her head, amused.

Chapter 19

The Monday morning after the fashion show, the stationary bike was going at a full clip as Angelique peddled, sweat drenching her workout clothes. Though she wore ear buds and listened to an Ann Jeffries audio novel, her eyes were riveted on Gregory as he ran on the treadmill. He wore a headset, no shirt, loose-fitting workout shorts and running shoes without socks. Moisture glistened on his upper body and the gold chain around his neck that read FAMILY matted to his light, brown-sugar, skin tone.

He looked absolutely, indescribably delicious with his well-toned body on display. He had a fluidity to his stride while he watched the reader board, the Business Channel, and carried on an intense business conversation on a telephone headset. Earlier she listened to him give a lecture to a college class somewhere in South Carolina and answer questions from the students all while lifting free weights. Occasionally, he would call in buy or sell orders via the laptop on his dashboard. No sooner would he complete one task than he would start another. Yet, his strides never faltered, but were, in her view, poetry in motion.

She marveled at how focused he was and believed he would bring the same level of intensity to the bedroom. Though she was eager to experience lovemaking with him, she appreciated his resolve not to take her to his bed at this juncture of their deepening relationship. He wasn't willing to jump into an affair which might prove unfulfilling for one or both of them. For now she understood the logic of his position. For him it wasn't about sex. He was unwilling to let his needs for sex lead the way.

"What are you thinking so intently about?" Gregory asked.

She hadn't noticed he watched her in the mirrored wall. "You don't want me to answer that when you're already half-dressed and sensually sweaty."

He smiled indulgently. "I'll take care of it momentarily," he said, as he slowed the treadmill to a walk for his cool-down cycle.

"No need to dress on my account," she teased. "I happen to like it when you're wet and warm from exercising." She slowed her stationary bike and shut off her audiobook.

"You're not half bad yourself," he said, toweling off the sweat. Then he gripped both ends of the towel hanging around his neck and watched her approach him with a lusty grin around her mouth.

"Which half would that be?" She eased up to him putting her arms around his neck.

"You're asking for trouble, Angelique," he said, as her body rubbed against his.

"You noticed?"

He laughed, disentangled her from him and slung an arm around her shoulders. "Have you completed the plans for Joyce's bridal shower?"

"I have, yes. Everything is arranged. What about you? Is everything done for Peter's bachelor party?"

"Yes. Surprisingly, a number of our friends from college plan to attend."

"When can we leave for DC for Christmas?"

"I think we can go right after I finish my duties as best man and the wedding is over. It's not a long drive from Monroe County, Pennsylvania, to Washington, DC."

"Let's hope the weather cooperates."

They turned off the lights in the gym and started for the stairs.

"How about a swim before lunch?"

"Sounds good to me. Then I'll make lunch."

"You don't want to go out somewhere?"

"I like being here. We have everything we need to make soup, salad, and sandwiches."

"All right, we'll swim and ..." Gregory paused when the front doorbell chimed.

They weren't expecting anyone and were surprised to see Slade Richardson on the security monitor.

"This is a surprise," said Angelique when Gregory let the handsome man enter.

"A pleasant one, I believe."

"Come in and have a seat. You have news?"

"Yes, we do. The threat to Ms. Menendez-Gaza and others is over."

Gregory and Angelique sat staring at Richardson.

"How did this happen?"

"The security breach you discovered to Ms. Menendez-Gaza's home and business was actually the tip of a very big iceberg. There was a criminal network in existence selling intimate access to famous people to clients and customers worldwide. The organization was not above kidnapping for a fee if the client wanted it.

"An attempt was made to kidnap Ms. Menendez-Gaza for a client. We, along with the FBI, CIA, Homeland Security, Interpol, and other law enforcement agencies in many countries were able to thwart their efforts and follow the links back to the source. The criminals were located in some renegade-run countries on the watch list. The organization and the clients have been neutralized, arrested, and detained on silent warrants executed by Interpol and issued by the World Court in The Hague.

"You're free to return to your normal life."

That bit of news should have thrilled her, but somehow, as her eyes met Gregory's, she felt an incredible sadness come over her.

"We've installed new state-of-the-art security in your flat, restaurant and bar. I'd like to take you home and walk you through the computer program Kenneth has devised for you."

"I'd appreciate it. If you don't mind waiting, I'd like to shower and change my clothes. I also need to pack my things."

"Take all the time you need."

"Thank you. I won't be long," she said, as she rose from her seat and rushed up the stairs. She didn't want anyone to see the tears she was desperately trying to hold back.

"How did this come about?" Gregory questioned Slade when Angelique was out of earshot.

"We picked up Stanton Durant, III, when he continued to try to find Ms. Menendez-Gaza. He claimed he was actually trying to warn her his parents were behind her security breach. Apparently, his father descended from Sir William Hamilton, British ambassador to Naples, his wife, Lady Emma Hamilton, and her lover, the naval hero Admiral Horatio Lord Nelson. The family has a long documented history of ménage à trois.

"Durant's mother's ancestry includes Georgiana, Duchess of Devonshire, the Duke of Devonshire and Lady Elizabeth Foster. Both of Durant's parents, much to the chagrin of The Royals, have practiced polyamory. They were both infatuated with Ms. Menendez-Gaza and encouraged Durant to bring her to them to form a foursome. When he refused, they began plotting to have her abducted and brought to one of their homes in Devonshire."

"This is very hard to believe. I've read that poet Ezra Pound and his wife Dorothy Shakespeare and their mistress, concert violinist Olga Rudge, who died in Youngstown, Ohio, in 1996, were in a three-way committed relationship until their deaths, but I didn't think it was still practiced in this day and time."

"We found many instances of polygamy involving one woman and two 'husbands'. Not all of the situations were voluntary. That was true of polygyny with one male and two or more females as well. We were able to help break up a major abduction ring trafficking in young girls and boys. We believe the backbone of this particular group has been identified and captured, but by no means have we been able to eliminate all of the factions. There are certain Middle Easterners, particularly in Oman, who are still being surveilled. There is suspicion other notables are involved but remain unindicted, co-conspiriters at this time. Still, we're actively keeping an eye on them."

Gregory winced at the thought any of his young nephews, nieces or cousins would be preyed on in such a despicable way. He listened to Richardson recount other atrocities which were unearthed and despaired of what might have happened to Angelique if Alondra hadn't asked him to have dinner with her; had he not been stuck in traffic outside of Angelique's restaurant which led to him finding the spyware on her computer and in her home. If all or any of those events changed, she might have just disappeared as others had without a trace.

He turned as did Richardson when the elevator bell chimed and Angelique stepped out burdened with lots of luggage.

"Let me help you with that," said Richardson as he relieved her of most of her bags.

When he left the house, Angelique turned to Gregory. "I believe I have everything."

"You're only across the city; not on the other side of the world. If you've forgotten something, I'll bring it to you or you can come back to get it. You're always welcomed here."

"Then I guess this is goodbye."

"All goodbyes aren't gone, Angel Face. Don't look so sad."

She went easily into his warm embrace holding him tight. "To be continued then?"

He caressed her cheek and lifted her chin for a kiss. "Yes, definitely, to be continued," he said, with an engaging grin.

About the Author

Ann Jeffries, the critically acclaimed author of the Family Reunion—Wisdom of the Ancestors Series, is a native of Washington, DC. As an only child, she enjoyed the benefits of a private school education at Allen in Asheville, North Carolina, and a public education at the University of Maryland. Ann began writing fiction for her own amusement.

Ms. Jeffries is the recipient of many awards for leadership and public service. A keynote speaker at colleges, universities, conferences, and conventions, she has extensively traveled the North American continent, Asia, and Europe. Among other endeavors, she is an entrepreneur, an avid supporter of public television, a genealogist, and a voracious reader.

Her pride and joy are her family, particularly her Fabulous Four grands. She lives in Maryland and South Carolina.

Follow Ann on her website: www.annjeffries.net, Facebook @Ann Jeffries, on Twitter @Ann Jeffries and her publishing house site: www.newviewliterature.com. Her novels are available in both e-book and paperback. Her autographed copies can be found through annjeffries.net and also un-autographed on Amazon.com and barnesandnoble.com.